Welfare Rights Work in Social Services

Geoff Fimister

M

MACMILLAN
EDUCATION
in association
with the Child
Poverty Action Group

First published 1986

Published by
MACMILLAN EDUCATION LTD
Houndmills, Basingstoke, Hampshire RG21 2XS
and London
Companies and representatives
throughout the world

Printed in Hong Kong

British Library Cataloguing in Publication Data
Fimister, Geoff
Welfare rights work in social services.—
(Practical social work)
1. Welfare rights movement—Great Britain
2. Social workers—Great Britain 3. Public
welfare—Great Britain
I. Title   II. Child Poverty Action Group
III. Series
361.6'14'0941   HV245
ISBN 0-333-36308-6
ISBN 0-333-36309-4 Pbk

To Anne

PRACTICAL SOCIAL WORK

Series Editor: Jo Campling

BASW

Social work is at an important stage in its development. All professions must be responsive to changing social and economic conditions if they are to meet the needs of those they serve. This series focuses on sound practice and the specific contribution which social workers can make to the well-being of our society in the 1980s.

The British Association of Social Workers has always been conscious of its role in setting guidelines for practice and in seeking to raise professional standards. The conception of the Practical Social Work series arose from a survey of BASW members to discover where they, the practitioners in social work, felt there was the most need for new literature. The response was overwhelming and enthusiastic, and the result is a carefully planned, coherent series of books. The emphasis is firmly on practice, set in a theoretical framework. The books will inform, stimulate and promote discussion, thus adding to the further development of skills and high professional standards. All the authors are practitioners and teachers of social work representing a wide variety of experience.

JO CAMPLING

PRACTICAL SOCIAL WORK

Series Editor: Jo Campling

BASW

Contents

Foreword

Poverty is widespread in Britain and it is on the increase – particularly among families with children. At the same time, cuts in the National Insurance scheme and higher rents and health charges have meant that means-tested benefits are playing an increasingly central role in our income maintenance system. According to one estimate, nearly a quarter of the population, over twelve million people, receive a means-tested benefit – five or six times as many as in the early years of the welfare state. Many more are entitled to such benefits but are not claiming them.

It is the means-tested benefits which provide the greatest problems for claimants. It is increasingly difficult to navigate a path through the complex benefits maze. The biggest nightmare is supplementary benefit, which is supporting over seven million people – or the equivalent of the population of London.

This is the dismal context in which social workers and others employed by social services agencies are working. Many of their clients' problems are problems born of deprivation and hardship. Social services agencies cannot eradicate poverty but they have, in welfare rights, an important tool for at least mitigating its impact. Theoretical distinctions between 'real' social work and practical welfare rights work are untenable and break down in the real world of social work practice. Yet it is clear that most social workers are singularly ill-equipped to provide their clients with the practical advice and help they urgently need. Evidence drawn together in this book confirms that social workers frequently lack training and information back-up in this complex area, even while recognising their clients' need for expert help and support and wanting to improve their knowledge and skills.

This book should be invaluable to the many social services staff who find themselves in this frustrating position. Geoff Fimister has many years' experience of welfare rights work in a local authority context which inform the very practical advice he gives on how to establish a 'welfare rights resource' in social services agencies and on how a welfare rights input can reinforce and extend the role of the personal social services in confronting poverty. I hope that all those who read this book will be convinced of the necessity of such an approach and that it will encourage social services agencies generally to give higher priority to income maintenance issues. It is the very least that their clients deserve.

RUTH LISTER
Director
Child Poverty Action Group

ABBREVIATIONS

AMA	Association of Metropolitan Authorities
BASW	British Association of Social Workers
CCETSW	Central Council for Education and Training in Social Work
CSS	Certificate in Social Service
CQSW	Certificate of Qualification in Social Work
CPAG	Child Poverty Action Group
CAB	Citizens' Advice Bureau
DHSS	Department of Health and Social Security
EEC	European Economic Community
HMSO	Her Majesty's Stationery Office
LA	Local Authority
NALGO	National and Local Government Officers' Association
NHS	National Health Service
OT	Occupational Therapist
SCC	Specialist Claims Control
SSAC	Social Security Advisory Committee
SSD	Social Services Department (and Scottish Social Work Department)
WRO	Welfare Rights Officer

Preface

The question of the role of welfare rights work in social services is increasingly, and rightly, finding its way onto the agenda of social services agencies. This book aims to support and further such developments, to consider the issues and to outline the possibilities and pitfalls in a way which I hope will prove both of interest and of concrete use to practitioners, teachers and policy-makers alike.

I owe thanks to a number of people for their help in various ways. First and foremost, Newcastle upon Tyne Social Services Department has been a source of encouragement and practical help. I am most grateful to its Director, Brian Roycroft, for permission to use the Welfare Rights Service's facilities; to welfare rights officers Diane Jones, Iain Kitt and Bob Wellburn for various items of information cited in the text; and to Barbara Lumsden and Elaine Dodd for the skilful and speedy typing of spidery drafts. By way of reciprocation, papers based on individual chapters have been made available through the Newcastle Welfare Rights information service and seem to have met with a healthy interest.

A number of people have commented on drafts. I am especially grateful to David Bull and Quintin Oliver for their detailed comments on the whole of the first draft; while others who have made helpful observations on particular aspects or sections are Tony Bennett, Barry Clark, Anne Fimister, Pete McGavin, Steve McGrail, Roger Smith, Mary Widdes and John Veit Wilson. I would also like to thank Ruth Lister, who contributed the foreword; and all those who responded to requests for information and research findings cited in the text.

The end result is of course, for better or worse, my responsibility.

GEOFF FIMISTER

1

Introduction

The meaning of the term 'welfare rights' can be debated at length and to varying degrees of philosophical abstraction. I should like to begin by setting out briefly its meaning as it is used in this book, and I shall aim to be straightforward. First, as regards subject matter, I have adopted what is probably the most common usage of the term, meaning rights to *income*, with particular reference to social security and other cash welfare benefits, and to directly related issues such as fuel disconnections. That is, I have not sought to embrace the whole range of welfare law, which would have included, for example, housing and health. Certainly, there will be overlap with these fields (housing benefits; exemption from NHS charges) but we are concerned here primarily with the income rights approach.

'Welfare rights' are also treated in these pages as an aspect of a person's wider civil rights : that is, we are concerned with welfare rights as *entitlements* and not as some form of state-funded charity, regardless of whether the latter might be perceived as grudgingly or benignly bestowed. By this definition, welfare rights are not concerned only with the relief of poverty : the *prevention* of poverty, and indeed the achievement of positively desirable living standards, by means of clear, adequate and enforceable non-means-tested entitlements, may one day be seen as an elementary requirement of a properly civilised community. In the meantime, though, it is the poverty-relieving implications of welfare rights activity which render it of increasingly pressing relevance to the social services.

I should also elaborate on the term 'social services'. Many of the issues are discussed in this book in terms of the implications of welfare rights for field social workers in local authority social services departments (SSDs) (a term which I trust Scottish readers will forgive me for using, in the interests of brevity, to embrace social work departments north of the border). There are, though, similar or in some senses analogous staff working in other contexts for whom the issues can be just as pressing. For example, in their different ways, psychiatric social workers, residential social workers, social workers in voluntary organisations, probation officers, community workers and home helps will have need of, and can be channels for, welfare rights advice and information.

Anybody connected with the social services world, whether as practitioner, policy-maker or educator, is likely to be having a busy time in the 1980s, and can no doubt expect this state of affairs to continue for the foreseeable future. High unemployment and industrial decline have brought in their wake all manner of chaos, poverty and stress; more and more people have come to depend on inadequate and disorganised means-tested benefits; social workers' caseloads increasingly feature redundancies, debt, bad housing and family break-up; social services agencies themselves have come up against Government public expenditure policies leading to anything from an irritating stationery famine to an alarming queue of unfilled social worker posts. In such a highly pressured climate as this, surely it is becoming ever harder to justify sitting down and reading a book (to say nothing of writing one)?

Nevertheless, I hope that in a real sense, whether as an aid to policy-making, to teaching or to practice, this book will repay the effort involved both in reading and writing it. This hope is fuelled by my conviction as to the central role which welfare rights issues must play in any organisation or set of circumstances substantially concerned with economic and social deprivation. The personal social services are up against welfare rights issues in a big way, whether they like it or not. Moreover, a wide range of client groups is involved, including elderly, sick and disabled people as well as the growing numbers of single parents and the unemployed.

A few moments' consideration of just some of the day-to-day concerns of the personal social services will illustrate the point: I have already referred to unemployment, poverty, debt, intolerable stresses and strains on the family. If we look at this a little more closely, we can specifically list rent arrears, evictions, fuel disconnections, missing social security giros, lost housing benefit certificates, unclaimed or wrongly refused benefits of all shapes and sizes, aggressive 'claims control' – a whole range of factors which exert pressure on individuals and families. The relationship is increasingly acknowledged between such adverse life circumstances and crises such as non-accidental injury to children or to frail or elderly dependants, reception into care, family break-up, mental breakdown, delinquency and crime. Wherever one places the emphasis – for example, whether one regards such pressures as creating such crises, or rather as exposing already vulnerable individuals to further risk – it is difficult to argue that the relationship is not there.

On a less dramatic level, many familiar policy-making or practical situations involve welfare rights considerations. Resettlement of mentally handicapped people into the community, whether as a planned programme or in an individual case, will involve questions of income support, as will the departure of young people from residential care: in the inhospitable environment of temporary 'training' schemes and large scale youth unemployment, sinking or swimming may well depend on how effectively the errant giro can be restored, or the elusive furniture grant wrung out of the system.

All of these circumstances present a challenge to the welfare rights capabilities of social services agencies. How well is your organisation equipped to tackle the 'welfare rights' dimension of these policy areas and practical difficulties? Do you have a good information system? Or do you have an incomplete and/or out-of-date set of leaflets, with perhaps a well-thumbed, coffee-stained 1978 edition of what should be this year's *CPAG National Welfare Benefits Handbook?* Are staff of your agency plugged into a reliable and regular in-service training programme; or did they once have a lecture on post-war social administration from old Entwistle at the Poly? Do they give clients sound advice with confidence; or doubtful advice with fingers crossed? Does your organisation have a worked-out *policy* for welfare rights; or do you hope that some keen young radical social worker will have time to 'mug up' during his or her annual leave and spread the word round the office?

These dilemmas and contrasts may be familiar to you. You may be a manager with a good information and training system but an interest in improving it; you may be an educator, seeking better links between your welfare rights course and the application of its message in the field; you may be the enthusiastic social worker referred to above, anxious for evidence with which to win over to the welfare rights cause an indifferent or even hostile management. Whoever you are, I hope you will find something useful in this book.

One role which the book is *not* intended to play is that of a welfare rights guide. It will not tell you, for example, how to calculate supplementary benefit entitlement. Welfare rights guides are discussed in Chapter 5. A related point concerns the extent to which examples given in the text will be 'up-to-date' in terms of the detailed provisions of social security and welfare benefit legislation current at the time of reading. The benefit system is notorious for the rapidity with which it mutates. I may well refer to a benefit − say, housing benefit supplement − which will have been modified or abolished by the time this book appears. The point is that examples are used here to illustrate principles, rather than detailed provisions.

I shall also attempt to strike a balance between the theoretical and the practical. There will be a substantial emphasis on the practicalities of setting-up specialist welfare rights resources, information systems and training programmes; but the intention is to locate them within a theoretical context, which will embrace some relatively controversial issues such as the place of welfare rights in social work.

The extent to which the arguments are applicable outside the English context also needs to be considered. In a sense, given the very widespread incidence of poverty and extent of social security systems and personal social services activity, I would hope that the book would be of relevance to readers working in a variety of different social and cultural contexts.

On the more specific level, however, the arguments here are developed around the framework of the relevant English systems and institutions. Most of them are also readily applicable elsewhere on the British mainland, albeit with some differences – partly of terminology – in Scotland. I am less confident as regards Northern Ireland, where there are significant institutional differences; and certainly, in other European countries, and in the United States and elsewhere, variations in traditions and attitudes (for example, as regards the role of social work in relation to poverty) may be expected to qualify some of the conclusions drawn. I have not endeavoured to embrace such considerations within the scope of the book, but they should be borne in mind.

The question of the place of welfare rights in social work is tackled first, in Chapter 2. There has been a good deal of debate of late concerning the proper relationship between the two disciplines: I should like to consider some of the issues and set out my own view of the subject.

Chapter 3 will pursue the argument that every social services agency should have, or have access to, a 'welfare rights resource', which may take different forms, depending on local circumstances, but which should be capable at least of servicing all relevant social services staff, and which will in many respects be the key to opening up a range of opportunities for training, advice and information. The particular role of the growing number of separate local authority welfare rights services provides a main focus for discussion of the possibilities for meeting these various requirements.

Being aware that a welfare rights resource is needed, and actually acquiring one, are of course two different matters. Acquisition of resources is a political question – not necessarily in a party political sense, but in terms of the decision-making processes which operate, formally and informally, within the local authority. Social services staff are, in my experience, often surprisingly innocent of such matters. Chapter 4 discusses the issues and seeks to outline some of the key political/bureaucratic advantages and obstacles which are likely to be encountered.

Chapter 5 deals with information systems. I shall not

be suggesting that you should kit out your area team sub-office as if it were a law centre. Nevertheless, there are important organisational and administrative questions associated with the running of reliable information systems, especially across a large department, where there may be a number of offices to service.

Chapter 6 deals with training. In a field which changes, as I have noted above, with disconcerting rapidity, continuing in-service training opportunities are essential. Possibilities for setting up such facilities are discussed, together with their relationship to initial training on qualifying courses.

Finally, some interesting questions surround the taking up of wider issues, perhaps tackling matters of local authority or even central government policy. This is a popular pursuit amongst welfare rights agencies as such, but is perhaps less conventional within mainstream social services traditions. Chapter 7 considers this area.

One final observation remains to be made in this introductory section. A number of the proposals put forward in this book (for example, for the appointment of welfare rights advisers, or the improvement of training and information systems) have resource implications for local authorities. Even if the agency concerned is in the non-governmental sector, local authority finance is very likely to be involved, through voluntary sector funding programmes. The public spending climate is, though, unfavourable towards the development of new initiatives. Local authorities are experiencing very major problems created by 'overspending' penalties and 'rate-capping'. Are we, then, merely indulging in wishful thinking in considering new initiatives in welfare rights? I think not. I hope that evidence presented in later chapters will convince the reader that a welfare rights approach, by generating extra income for often desperately hard-pressed claimants and their families, can be regarded as a highly cost-effective use of resources. Moreover, even where a local authority's resources are severely constrained, there can still be scope for some modest policy development, as priorities evolve in response to changing circumstances. I would not wish to exaggerate this point, especially at a time when many advice centres are under threat from insecure funding, but such factors nevertheless must surely explain why local authority 'in house' welfare rights provision, at least, has continued to develop in the 1980s in spite of the hostile financial climate ; and in some areas, voluntary sector funding also has been improved. As I have argued above, growing poverty and unemployment have pushed welfare rights firmly onto the social services agenda.

2

Welfare Rights and Social Work

A chapter concerned specifically with the question of welfare rights and social work seems essential because, although I have argued in Chapter 1 that social workers are not the only employees of social services agencies to whom the subject of welfare rights is, or should be, important, complicated and much-debated issues have arisen in relation to the particular position of social workers.

Why should social work attract so much attention in this context? We have noted that social workers are far from being the only group working in close contact with socially and economically deprived people, inside or outside the personal social services. The potential of workers such as occupational therapists, home helps and housing staff for involvement in welfare rights exercises is in fact beginning to attract more interest: but it is unlikely that such developments will excite the passions which surround the question of welfare rights and social work.

The reason for this is certainly partly because, while many people believe that social workers should be involved in welfare rights, the profession itself appears to be highly ambivalent about it. For example, the reaction of occupational therapists to news of the Islington experiment described later in this chapter, is likely to be : fine, but is it practicable? Whereas the reaction of the social work profession to the question of welfare rights in social work is frequently : is it philosophically sound?

This is not to say that I would necessarily accept the stereotype of the social worker as a psychologically-inclined avoider of material problems. My own observations suggest that there is a significant minority which is solidly in favour of welfare rights in social work, and a further group (perhaps potentially quite large) which would be in favour, given appropriate agency priorities and back-up resources – a point to which I shall return. Nevertheless, the philosophical anxiety is real and pervasive. There is no doubt that it derives its main origins from some of the historical tributaries of social work : neither the charitable nor the psychoanalytical currents within social work run very easily alongside structural explanations of poverty or an emphasis on the vigorous affirmation of rights. Moreover, this very ideological diversity contributes to a climate of uncertainty as to what exactly is the 'social work task'. This leads to a lack of clarity on issues such as the role of welfare rights.

Thus, while it seems to me that various contemporary approaches to social work could in fact fit in rather well with a welfare rights approach, the subject can be avoided or neglected. The Barclay Report (1982) is an example of this. As David Bull (1982b, p.11) puts it, current debate on the role of welfare rights in social work is taking place

> in the aftermath of a report on the social worker's role that has done more to confuse than to advance our analysis : the tasks of 'advice'; 'advocacy'; 'brokerage'; 'mediation'; and 'negotiation' were sometimes mentioned interchangeably, sometimes loosely distinguished, but never adequately defined and delimited by the Barclay Committee.

The Barclay Committee's skirting of this issue has also been noted in the context of consumer research, which suggests that clients themselves have fairly definite views on the place of material questions. Summarising various findings, Becker, MacPherson and Silburn (1983, p.52) conclude that:

> Consumer research has shown that favourable assessments of social work occur where material problems are tackled as the most pressing problem. Barclay found that what really mattered for clients was that the social worker had ... tangible knowledge about local facilities and services. Clients were not on the whole particularly impressed by or even aware of the more esoteric social work skills. Curiously, whilst welfare rights work would fit well into such a client's perspective, it was not explicitly mentioned in the Barclay report.

The overlap between poverty, social work and welfare rights is, of course, extensive. To point out that some of the main groups which figure large in social workers' case-loads – families of single parents, the unemployed, the low-paid; sick and disabled and elderly people – are also the groups most vulnerable to poverty, is hardly to make an original observation. To point out that these are the main groups dependent upon social security benefits and potentially in need of welfare rights advice and support is even more obvious.

I do not intend to labour this point unnecessarily : as Robert Holman (1980, p.14) puts it, referring to reception of children into public care : 'To some, the relationship between poverty (or social deprivation) and child separation may seem so obvious as to need no discussing'. Several years earlier, Olive Stevenson (1973, p.29) observed that : 'The interaction of the different aspects of human need – material, social and psychological – is obvious. Social work is, by definition, concerned with these interactions and this concern gives it its distinctive character'.

Obvious or not, I would nevertheless like to set the scene by drawing a little more on the observations of Holman and others, to emphasise these crucial interconnections. Summarising some of the main pieces of evidence on poverty and family break-up, Holman comments:

> The children of the poor are more likely than other sections of the population to be taken away from their parents. The reasons cannot simply and wholly be attributed to personality or family interaction as though these occurred quite separately from the environment. The inequality which is revealed in their lack of access to income, housing, health, education and so on is also shown in a greater probability that they will lose their families.

He goes on to remark that poverty promotes

> three further deprivations which can impair family behaviour. First, the poor are more liable to physical ill-health which, in turn, can seriously impair parenting capacites. Second, the poor may be denied the prerequisites for normal child socialisation activities. They lack indoor space, outside play facilities, books, outings and educational toys, all of which stimulate intellectual and social growth. Third, parents may be deprived of self-respect and a positive self-image. In our society, such feelings

depend on being able to participate, on being able to contribute as well as to take...Frequently, deprived persons receive such low incomes that acts of repayment are curtailed. They cannot return a material kindness, perhaps not purchase a decent present for their children within the exchange of family relationships. Unable to provide, unable to participate in normal life, perhaps handicapped by ill-health, the poor are made to feel inferior. (Holman, 1980, pp.16 – 17)

Equality for Children is an umbrella group bringing together a number of bodies (including, for example, the British Association of Social Workers (BASW), Child Poverty Action Group (CPAG), Commission for Racial Equality and National Council for One Parent Families) concerned with public policy relating to families and children. Commenting on the evidence submitted by various agencies, in 1982 – 3, to the House of Commons Social Services Select Committee's investigation into the question of children in care, Equality for Children (1983, p.4) observed:

At times poverty is the clear cause of reception into care. More frequently it precipitates families to act in ways which may be deemed irresponsible, feckless or pathological. Poverty severely curtails the opportunities for families to overcome life crises, or purchase respite from insidious daily pressure. To us, poverty and the resulting limitation to life chances was the most obvious thread linking the various submissions to the Select Committee.

One could make similar points concerning the disruption of rehabilitative work with the mentally ill, due to absence of furniture or to long delays in paying housing benefit. Even assuming that such clients would be in quite such a mental and emotional mess in the first place, were they financially better off (some would, of course), the relationship between relapse and lack of bank balance becomes starkly apparent in such circumstances. The health and safety of the elderly, the price of fuel and the level of benefits is another such notorious interaction.

Poverty is, then, clearly closely tied up with a range of social work concerns, and it is therefore very difficult to argue that social work is not firmly up against welfare rights issues. The question which concerns us here, though, is : what is the relationship between social work and welfare rights *work*? Is it possible to argue that, fully recognising the above connections, it is nevertheless not the task of social workers to become involved in the welfare rights aspects of the problem?

Arguments against welfare rights in social work

Bull (1982a, pp.5 – 9) and Becker, MacPherson and Silburn (1983, pp.54 – 63) have listed various arguments which are commonly advanced in support of such a thesis. My list of the arguments which I have encountered is fairly similar to theirs, although I have come across one or two others to add to the collection. Such arguments tend to take the form either that welfare rights work would be done better and/or more appropriately by some other body; or even that it is actively undesirable for social workers to undertake such work. (I am not concerned here with arguments which some non-enthusiasts might advance against welfare rights work being undertaken by anybody.) Some of these arguments have also been deployed to oppose the appointment of specialist welfare rights officers (WROs) in SSDs, so, although WROs are largely considered in Chapter 3, I shall include this particular aspect of that discussion here. The main arguments against social workers' involvement in welfare rights which I would like to consider are as follows.

'Welfare rights work is not part of "real" social work.'

This begs the question of what 'real' social work actually is, and it has been pointed out above that the lack of consensus within the profession muddies the waters.

Writing in the early 1970s, Jane Streather (1972, p.3) describes a social work client, a single parent of ten children who had been unknowingly struggling below the supplementary benefit level, and asks: '. . . what about preventive social work? In [this case] lack of income resulted in persistent rent arrears with the risk of rendering the family homeless with all that that implies in terms of human misery, financial cost to the community and use of scarce social work resources'. She goes on to declare herself firmly on the side of those who believe, with Barbara Wootton (1959, p.296), that

> the complexity of relevant rules and regulations has become so great, that the social worker who has mastered these intricacies and is prepared to place knowledge at the disposal of the public, and when necessary to initiate appropriate action has no need to pose as a miniature psychoanalyst or psychiatrist : her professional standing is secured by the value of her own contribution.

I shall argue later in this chapter that a minimum level of knowledge and skill is essential to avoid the failure even to identify a problem (leaving aside the question of cure). However, there are also strong arguments as to why a degree of welfare rights involvement is likely to be of value in strengthening (and indeed, avoiding damage to) the relationship between client and social worker, whatever the definition of social work.

Roger Smith, in CPAG's submission to Barclay, describes an example of a probation officer's failure to identify a relatively straightforward means of tackling his client's fuel debt problem. He observes that this case

> illustrates two points. The first is that the possibility, if not probability of a link between a client's objective and subjective state cannot be be avoided. The woman who telephoned us was distraught and clearly suffering a large degree of stress. Restoration of electricity may well not have been the answer to all her problems though it clearly was to one of them and it may well have made her more receptive towards working to a solution to any others. The second point is that a social worker needs in many cases all the credibility that can be got when working within a difficult situation. This probation officer's client was describing her probation officer in unflattering terms. Her perception of his inability to give any assistance with her simple concrete problem was clearly going to affect her belief in him in any other context. (R.Smith, 1981, p.6)

Supporting this view, a social worker once put it to me that : 'You've got to help clients with their income problems...it helps you to build up trust...it's very unusual not to find something concrete you can do' (quoted in Fimister, 1981b, p.21). Or, as Ruth Cohen and Andree Rushton put it:

> The experience of success in claiming for rights and services will create confidence in the client that the social worker is effective and concerned. Problems may then emerge which the client has previously withheld and with which the social worker may be able to help. In this way, welfare rights work has a spin-off. How can a client feel confidence in a helper who is not interested in her practical problems? (1982, p.16)

'Social workers should not strain relations with other official agencies.'

Some readers may be tempted to dismiss this as weakness, collusion with bureaucracy or simply failing the client. Certainly, it seems to imply either that the client should be left to get on with it unaided or that somebody else should do the boat-rocking. However, it may also underestimate the sophistication of social security officers, who may in fact welcome informed advocacy to help 'sort out' a case. Certainly, there is evidence that such advocacy may be preferred to uninformed intervention : several commentators have argued, as has Bull (1982a, p.8), that 'we might ask whether it is the social worker's ignorance, rather than his opposition, which is the real bane of the challenged supplementary benefits officer'.

'Welfare rights work is too complex for the non-specialist.'

Welfare rights is indeed a notoriously complex area and one which changes rapidly. There is no escaping the fact that even specialists have their work cut out to keep up-to-date; so the problems facing non-specialists are considerable. This position has been much exacerbated by the 1980 and subsequent legislation in the supplementary and housing benefit fields. I shall not attempt to broach this extensive subject here : suffice it to say that, under the code-name 'simplification' (a government euphemism for 'reduction in the numbers of civil servants') there has been introduced a new legal basis to large areas of the benefit system, involving what Lynes (1981, p.18) calls 'a mass of fiendishly complicated regulations' which, moreover, are now changing more quickly than annually updated guides can keep pace.

Nevertheless, social workers who cite complexity as a reason for 'opting out', may find their motives suspected. An example is provided by an exchange in a social work journal which took place even before the 1980 legislation was passed. Later in this chapter, I shall describe a successful benefit take-up project at a training centre for mentally handicapped people in Harlow. Writing this up in *Community Care*, Tony Bennett and Pete McGavin (1980a, p.19) commented that 'advising the disabled on their entitlement is not such a specialist job that it needs a welfare rights officer to do it. Any social worker could help a handicapped person claim the allowances mentioned in this article'. This sparked off a lively exchange in the letters columns between P. Smith, a reader from Doncaster, and Bennett and McGavin:

> The suggestion that social services departments can accomplish improved take-up through social workers is merely a recommendation that SSDs should present another second-rate service, and undervalues the vital work being accomplished in other welfare rights settings. All SSD clients should have access to a professional in the field of welfare rights, just as they should for a 'social work' problem. (P.Smith, 1980)

This rather begs the question of whether such a 'social work' problem can be disentangled from its welfare rights elements. In any case, Bennett and McGavin (1980b) are having none of this. Such comments, they reply, 'only arouse our suspicions that the social workers' cry of "too difficult – call the experts" when faced with a benefit problem is little more than a rationalisation of a narrow approach to casework'. They point out that in the real world, the ready availability of a skilled welfare rights adviser to all citizens in need of such support is a long way away; and they insist again that there is much potential for social workers to help secure their clients' welfare rights.

My own view is that, while it may be true that social workers cannot necessarily be expected to engage in highly sophisticated displays of welfare advocacy on a regular basis, there is evidence – some of it cited below – to suggest that much can be achieved, complexity notwithstanding. However, such an approach, if it is to be a realistic prospect, must command management support, a suitable place in agency priorities, and adequate training and information back-up. These factors are central themes of this book.

'Some other agency should handle welfare rights.'

As noted above, this belief can stem from a view that there is
something intrinsically wrong with social workers'
involvement; or simply that other agencies would do it better
or more appropriately. Sometimes these arguments merely
serve unintentionally to demonstrate that there is a good case
for a wide range of agencies to be involved in welfare rights as
well as, rather than instead of, social services bodies. I would
like to focus here, though, on three particular 'branches' of
the 'some other agency should do it' approach : that in which
genuine procedures for referral to relevant bodies are
established; that in which the alternative agency is
unspecified; and that which maintains that the benefit-
administering agency should itself be responsible for welfare
rights work.

(a) 'Cases should be referred on in an organised way.'   As
long as the necessary minimum level of welfare rights skill
needed for effective identification of problems is borne in
mind, it seems to me that there is no fundamental reason why
more detailed welfare rights intervention should not be
achieved by referral to other agencies, provided that the
referral process is well organised, and that the alternative
agency actually exists (which, as I shall argue below, is not
always the case). The social work agency will, of course,
thereby lose the advantage of being able to offer certain types
of valuable service to its clients, but as long as the referral
process works, and somebody is providing the necessary
service to the claimant, then this sort of model is at least
defensible, if not necessarily that which I (and certainly not
the 'prescriptive' school discussed below) would advocate.

It should be stressed, though, that this approach requires a
good knowledge of agencies undertaking welfare rights work
and how to refer cases to them. (Some of the consequences of
poor referral practices are discussed in Chapter 5.) This
means regular communications with such agencies,
preferably including periodic meetings to discuss current

relevant issues and to monitor the effectiveness of the 'network'. Relevant bodies could be local authority, voluntary sector or other 'non-governmental' advice centres, claimants' unions and so on, but a clear understanding of what services are on offer and how to refer is required all round.

(b) 'Cases should be referred on to. . . er. . . somebody.' This approach entails the same decision as above, to refer a case on for welfare rights action, but without any of the homework as to alternative sources of help. It should be borne in mind, of course, that different approaches may be adopted by different social workers within the same agency (a point discussed further below) and so even where the agency has worked-out referral procedures, individuals may not be taking sufficient account of them. However, it is possible for *agency* policy to adopt the 'refer on, we know not where' approach. In its most extreme form, this is little more than an irresponsible dodging of the issue: but there are milder forms, and these seem very common. This includes, for example, the vague injunction to visit an advice centre, without bothering about opening times, and other malpractices described in Chapter 5.

(c) 'The DHSS should do it.' The view that, in the event of a disagreement over entitlement, the best person to advise the claimant is the other party to the dispute, is on the face of it so odd that it is surprising to find it so frequently held. I have described this elsewhere as 'roughly akin to asking a player in one of the teams at a football match to double as referee' (Fimister, 1977, p.8). David Bull has nevertheless 'encountered this position at a dangerously high level of social services management' (1982b, p.11). In their study of 170 social workers in Nottinghamshire, Becker, MacPherson and Silburn (1983, p.38, Table 4.5) found that ten respondents thought DHSS should be primarily responsible for advocacy. I am not sure whether to be pleased that there were only ten, or depressed that anybody should hold to what, in Bull's words (1982a, p.6) might be thought an 'especially facile argument'.

But if such a view is so facile, why does it survive? The cause probably lies in a confusion between, on the one hand, the responsibility of benefit-administering agencies to publicise their wares and administer them efficiently; and on the other, the claimant's need for independent advice and support in the event of a problem or disagreement. This confusion is no doubt compounded by the fact that both welfare rights and benefit-administering agencies may engage in, and even collaborate over, benefit publicity exercises of one sort or another; while good liaison arrangements on individual cases may also convey a collaborative image. (This is indeed one of the drawbacks of the DHSS 'liaison officer' system : it can lead the unwary to allow a friendly relationship to blunt a full insistence on the claimant's case.) For these reasons, there is a need to press home firmly the point that the DHSS, as a party to any potential disagreement, cannot provide independent advice and advocacy. (The problem where the local authority is itself the benefit-administering agency is discussed in Chapter 3, as it is a difficulty which has particularly presented itself recently in relation to WROs and housing benefit.)

'Computers should do it.'

A number of local authorities and other bodies, such as the DHSS and certain Citizens' Advice Bureaux, are rightly exploring the uses of modern computer technology in benefit information (and administration). This is an area in which there is likely to be rapid progress in the next few years. There are still many 'bugs', but also much potential. Nevertheless, while computers can assess entitlements, it is much less clear how far they can effectively 'interview' claimants: interactive systems are being explored (see for example Ballantyne, 1984) and it may be expected that both the public and the computers will become more used to dealing with each other in the future. Nevertheless, the more complicated 'conversations' will be beyond the reach of current possibilities; and certainly, the prospect of computers negotiating with the DHSS, fuel boards and so on, or representing at tribunals, is too futuristic a vision for our present purposes. Thus, computers can provide only part of a welfare rights strategy.

'Welfare rights work should be conducted via take-up campaigns, which reach more people than individual advisers.'

Take-up campaigns can certainly form a useful part of a welfare rights strategy – but again, only a part. They have sometimes been thought of as an alternative to welfare rights workers: but in fact skilled advisers are needed to plan, organise and run them; and a large-scale campaign in an area which lacks an adequate 'infrastructure' of advice centres will generate a large demand for follow-up support which cannot be met. It may thus actually increase the demand for help from social workers as well as from welfare rights specialists.

The argument about 'reaching more people' must also take into account the contribution of 'cause advocacy' (see below) which aims to achieve favourable changes for whole groups of claimants.

'Clients should do it themselves.'

There are two main variants of this approach: that claimants' own organisations, rather than middle-class professionals, should handle welfare rights work; or that individual claimants should handle the work themselves.

The view that claimants' own organisations – self-help groups such as, for example, claimants' unions or single parents' groups – should be responsible for welfare rights work, rests on a desire to avoid what is seen as an undignified dependency on the part of the claimant: self-organisation replaces reliance on the professional. Hilary Rose, commenting on supplementary benefit appeal tribunals, observed in 1973 that:

> There is a tendency for a form of middle-class co-option to emerge, whereby the educated and the expert enter into a compassionate complicity, where the chairman and the well-briefed middle-class representative retreat into an expert's world, leaving the appellant no longer an actor in his own

destiny but merely the object of the case at issue. (Rose, 1973, p.411)

While Rose's approval of the self-help approach is made clear, she does not enter into the question of whether or not this can or should be the only form of welfare rights provision available to claimants. Nor does she seek to deal with the role of the welfare rights officer (a very rare animal in 1973). Nevertheless, John Barter (1973a, p.389) hijacks her thesis to argue against the appointment of WROs:

> The Claimants' Union achieves victories and at the same time enhances the self-esteem of appellants in a way forever denied to middle-class advocates. As a solid case against the vogue for appointing welfare rights officers, Hilary Rose's paper will take a lot of beating. It lends weight to those who feel that it is virile self-help groups which are more likely to ensure welfare, civil, *and* moral rights.

And (1973b, p.511): 'If a choice has to be made between spending money on welfare rights workers or in promoting angry, self-help groups, it may be better to invest in the latter.'

The case in favour of self-help groups undertaking welfare rights work is strong, and I support it. Nevertheless, the argument as advanced by Barter is too abstract compared with what is likely to happen in reality, especially in the context of the 1980s. There is certainly no reason why self-help groups should not be able to develop sound advice and advocacy services for their members: but they will face the same problems of time, training and information systems as anybody else. (The occasionally-expressed view that it is OK for self-help groups to get it wrong, provided that they are sufficiently angry, is in my view both patronising and irresponsible. It is indeed likely to make the claimants concerned angry – but not with the system.) Such groups are therefore quite likely to approach the local authority for funds, possibly towards expenses, possibly to employ staff. In the real world, self-help groups are part of the 'advice network': they sometimes employ 'full-timers', they purchase information material and attend and contribute to training programmes. It can often be difficult to distinguish a WRO with the right attitude from a skilled adviser who is a member of a self-help group.

This brings me onto the question of whether there is really something intrinsically undignified about having a salaried adviser handle your case. Here, it is necessary to distinguish between social workers and rights workers. Rights workers have it easier in this respect, in that they can make the straightforward and in my view entirely sound point that citizens are entitled to good advice services, and rich people do not seem to feel too humiliated about their own considerable dependence on their solicitors and accountants. Barbara Wootton (1959, p.296) once made this point in relation to social workers : but social workers cannot escape the ambivalence inherent in their simultaneously supportive and controlling roles. Rights workers, solicitors and accountants do not have statutory powers to take children into care or sanction compulsory admissions into mental hospitals. There is no escaping the fact that an element of stigma is involved in 'needing social work help'. This is not an argument, though, against social workers' involvement in welfare rights. Certainly, it is an argument against regarding social work offices as substitutes for advice centres (see below), but as regards those who approach social work agencies for help, or indeed who are involuntarily involved with SSDs, the more practical the help provided, the more concretely useful it seems to be from the consumer's point of view, the less is likely to be the stigma attached to social work services.

The argument that *claimants as individuals* should 'do it themselves' is far less sound than the case for self-help groups. This approach is sometimes encountered as a less sophisticated version of the 'anti-dependency' position described above, and derives from a radical, if badly thought-out, perspective. Another version, though, stems from highly patronising notions concerning claimants' 'standing on their own feet'. Quintin Oliver, then of Strathclyde Regional Council's Welfare Rights Service, has reported that 'we have had cases where social workers have objected to our rights officers representing their clients at tribunals because they were expected to stand up for themselves as part of their treatment plan. That is real paternalism!' (Quoted in Sharron, 1982, p.8).

I have argued above that social security is a highly complex subject; and against the idea that paid, professional welfare rights support is stigmatising. Those points are relevant here. Bull's citation of Monty Python's 'How to Take your Appendix Out on the Piccadilly Line', as his 'favourite satirical comment on the excesses of the self-sufficiency school' (1982a, p.7) is mischievous but fair comment.

This is not to suggest, though, that claimants as individuals do not have a role to play in pursuing their own cases. There is a spectrum of needs and wishes here, ranging from claimants who need no more than access to a handbook and a telephone, to those who want virtually the whole case to be handled by the adviser. The choice should ultimately be made by the claimant, in the light of whatever explanations and encouragement (but not pressure) may be appropriate. In between the extremes there are, as several commentators have pointed out, various degrees of sharing of the case between adviser and claimant. Becker, for example, makes this point (1983, p.50); as does Bull, who also points to the element of *reciprocity* involved where the claimant permits his or her experiences to be used as evidence in support of wider advocacy of a particular cause (1982a, p.8).

The policy of my own agency, Newcastle Welfare Rights Service, is that claimants who use our services are citizens and voters who have a *right to expect* a good, efficient, skilled service which will maximise their chances of winning their claim. They also have a right to expect to be able to participate in that process to whatever extent they wish, no more and no less. They should have to put up neither with exclusion by an overbearing professional, nor with neglect of their case by a sanctimonious consciousness-raiser.

The main arguments against welfare rights in social work are, then, diverse and of varying degrees of intellectual robustness. They are, of course, not necessarily discrete categories of argument: they can combine and overlap, sometimes in a rather complex fashion. Even ideas which should be mutually exclusive can combine, reflecting a deep ambivalence towards this issue. For example, the 'complexity' argument – the idea that welfare rights is too specialised a subject to be effectively 'taken on board' by social workers – can sometimes combine with a simultaneous and perhaps contradictory feeling that there is something more mundane about money advice which does not require such esoteric skills as those of the social work profession (a version of the 'not real social work' theme). Sometimes, there may be a worked-out idea here that welfare rights is a complex but ultimately earthy skill; but more often I suspect that it is a defensive reaction, born of the 'knowledge overload' faced by the generic social worker who is haunted by the feeling that he or she should have, or may be expected to have, a command of the more obscure recesses of the social security legislation. One such apparently ambivalent juxtaposition is provided by Robert Pinker's discussion in *New Society,* some years ago, of the proper boundaries of social work:

> social workers [also] perform a multitude of *straightforward practical tasks* on behalf of their clients: they give information and advice; they provide liaison with other agencies such as the housing and the social security services; and they sometimes act as advocates of welfare rights...It is not surprising that most practising social workers are dispirited by the impossibility of achieving all that is expected of them...In my view, any serious extension of social work practice into the general field of welfare rights must do irreparable damage not only to the credibility of social workers but also to the welfare rights of their clients. The legislation affecting rights (and obligations) in any field of social service, whether housing or social security, is *so complex* that intervention by amateurs – apart from referring clients to experts – is likely to do more harm than good. (Pinker, 1979, p.595 [author's emphasis])

On this analysis, then, welfare rights is a 'straightforward practical task' which is 'so complex' that intervention by social workers 'is likely to do more harm than good' – ambivalence indeed!

I would like now to consider further the arguments in favour of social workers' involvement in welfare rights work.

Arguments in support of welfare rights in social work

A number of these have, of course, emerged already from my comments on the arguments against. However, I would like to elaborate on some of these and to introduce certain others. I would like to begin, though, by considering the key question of *minimum standards*.

Minimum standards

Cohen and Rushton, firm advocates of the application of welfare rights methods to social work, link the former to a variety of different approaches to the latter, pointing out their relevance to Seebohm-style genericism, radical social work, the unitary approach, family therapy, task-centred methods, and so on (Cohen and Rushton, 1982, pp.15 – 16). These are all valid points, but I do not propose to pursue the argument along such diverse paths. It seems to me that the case for social workers involving themselves in welfare rights to at least the minimum levels which I discuss below, rests on much more straightforward considerations.

Given the close interrelationships of the variety of problems with which social workers deal and various manifestations of material deprivation, I would argue that it is not possible credibly to maintain that welfare rights considerations are not relevant to the well being of social workers' clients. It is still possible to maintain that it is not the social worker's job to take action on such issues; but if the social worker is to 'refer on' responsibly, then a level of welfare rights knowledge is required which is at least good enough to permit recognition that a problem exists and to permit diagnosis at least to the extent that a coherent referral can be made. To maintain otherwise is to condone the turning of a blind eye, by supposedly 'helping' professionals, to clients' often serious problems, and I do not believe that this is very easy to justify, morally or intellectually.

On the rare occasions when I have heard of specific defences of non-intervention to this extent, it has been in the context of the most unacceptable paternalism. I recall with a mixture of amusement and depression an incident involving a social work student on placement with Newcastle Welfare Rights Service. She was trying out her skills on our telephone advice line and, in pursuit of an enquiry from a claimant, had phoned the social worker involved in the case, concerning unclaimed benefit and possible steps which might be taken to help put matters right. Not only was the social worker unrepentant as to her own previous inaction, but she actually defended it on the grounds that her client (a widow of working age, if I remember rightly) needed to stand more on her own two feet, and that additional benefit would not encourage this. Perhaps not appreciating that our student was herself a social worker rather than a WRO she went on to observe sagely that there were differences between our two approaches. 'Yes,' replied our student through clenched teeth, 'we're on the client's side.'

Cohen and Rushton (1982, p.20) give a similar example where, this time, a social work student was the villain of the piece: 'one of us was told by a student that she would not wish to tell a certain client his rights to benefits as she felt he should find himself a job'.

Such attitudes are fortunately rare. My point is merely that it is only at the more eccentric extremes of non-intervention in a client's income entitlements that it can be argued that social workers do not need a level of welfare rights skill at least sufficient to ensure sound identification and reasonably accurate diagnosis of income problems.

If a certain minimum level of skill along such lines is required, we can only be concerned at the various pieces of evidence presented in this chapter which suggest powerfully that the absence of such skills is widespread. The problem is exacerbated by the fact that such is the nature of the benefit system, that even a minimum level of skill actually has to be quite high. Complexity can intrude into the most everyday cases. Thus, Roger Smith (1981, p.17) maintains that there is a '...difficulty in practice of dividing the problem of identification in the field of welfare benefits from a deeper knowledge of the field'; and goes as far as to argue that 'It may well be that only if you are familiar with the whole field of welfare rights through training, experience and practice can you be an adequate diagnostician'.

I would argue that there are gradations of skills above the minimum – it is not 'all or nothing' – but the level of skill necessary to achieve the minimum should not be underestimated.

Since pioneering work in Strathclyde, at an occupational and recreational centre for physically disabled people, demonstrated 'a massive shortfall in take-up of benefits' (Casserly and Clark, 1978, p.5), an increasing number of action research projects have confirmed a major problem of non-diagnosis of lost income amongst clients of the personal social services. Let us take, for example, Tony Bennett and Pete McGavin's work at the Pyenest Training Centre for mentally handicapped people, in Harlow : 'In all, 47 of the 100 trainees who took part in the survey received a total of 101 extra benefits, allowances or grants as a result of the survey...over a two-year period, trainees at the Pyenest Centre have gained entitlements of over £16 000....' They point out that:

> Those attending day centres, either for the physically or the mentally handicapped, are all in touch with a social services department, and most will have contact with a social worker. So these surveys raise the obvious question: can social workers and SSDs do anything more to ensure greater take-up of welfare benefits by the handicapped?

After outlining methods whereby entitlements to attendance and mobility allowances and supplementary benefit additional requirements could be identified in such a setting, they further make the telling observation that:

> Many families commented bitterly to us that they had been in contact with professionals such as social workers and health visitors for many years, but had not been informed about their benefits and rights. We feel that informing the handicapped about their benefits is a duty of the social worker. (Bennett and McGavin, 1980a, p.19)

A further example is provided by action research amongst mentally handicapped day centre attenders in Coventry, with particular reference to attendance allowance. Colin Blunn and Mick Small, specialist social workers for mentally handicapped people, discovered 83 clients (25 per cent) of those apparently eligible who were not claiming. Of these, 79 made successful claims as a result of the social workers' intervention. 'In economic terms, for people attending Coventry SSD's day centres for the mentally handicapped, the project has been a major success. At November 1983 rates of benefit we have been instrumental in the uptake of extra benefit equal to £100 000 per annum' (Blunn and Small, 1984).

Nor do Blunn and Small regard this as merely a financial transaction.

> Some individuals experienced a dramatic increase in their benefit (e.g. from £24.55 to £53.55 a week) and this, as well as improving the material standards of their lives, has consequent emotional impact. It is important for professionals to recognise that the provision of a (relatively) realistic level of benefit is as important as support services in helping families to care for their handicapped member.

Attendance and mobility allowances were the focus of recent work, this time with physiotherapists and occupational therapists (OTs), undertaken in Islington by Ruth Cohen. The SSD's community OTs and community health physiotherapists encouraged and supported claims by their clients:

> During just two months they helped the people they visited gain benefits worth £19 000 per year ... at the end of two months they reported that they were happy to go on helping their clients claim attendance and mobility allowance; they now realised that they could do this as part of their normal work. It seems that they are likely to come across about six claims a month: on a rough calculation, in one year this would result in 72 claims, for benefits worth between £68 000 and £101 000 a year.

Cohen points out that possible entitlement to these particular benefits can be identified on non-financial criteria, so income details and calculations are not required. Back-up for reviews and appeals was provided by welfare rights advisers, as was the offer of a detailed benefits check – which resulted in identification of further unclaimed benefits. 'Only two out of 26 people who agreed to discuss finances were receiving all they were entitled to and had no other problems or queries' (Cohen, 1983, pp.3 – 5).

The Rubery Hill Benefits Project in Birmingham returns us to the context of social work, although still in the health field and again illustrating the potential for work with other groups of staff. This project was run by the Rubery Hill Hospital's Rehabilitation Committee, with two Birmingham University social work students. It began with a two-day training course run by Birmingham Tribunal Unit and the Department of Social Administration at Birmingham University, which culminated in a discussion of how the information gathered on the course might be applied in practice. Practical efforts were supported by the two social work students during their three-month placements. Thirty-six staff volunteered for the course, including social workers, nurses and ward clerks. Ann Davis (1984, p.15) describes some of the results as follows:

> The community nurses and staff at the day hospital found a number of vulnerable people whose existence in the community had become even more precarious with the introduction of the housing benefit scheme. [Davis is referring here to the chaotic effects of the complex, anomalous and widely maladministered new housing benefit scheme introduced in 1983.] Many of these people had been known to hospital staff for years, but they had never taken the opportunity before to talk about benefit problems. . . Staff estimated that in dealing with queries from 39 patients, £2 800 was sent out by the DHSS in lump sum payments and an extra £200 a week was gained in enhanced benefit payments. Staff on the hospital's rehabilitation and long stay wards discovered that a number of their patients were entitled to partial attendance allowance. . . For some patients the extra income this benefit has given them has meant more regular contact with the family and the community.

Much of the action research which has been undertaken has thus focused on sick and disabled people, in hospital and day centre settings. It would be wrong, though, to suppose that the problem of unclaimed benefits is confined to the more specialised contexts. Advice centres regularly discover that underpaid claimants have had social workers for substantial periods. Certainly, the scope for action at the area team level has been shown by another piece of work carried out by Islington People's Rights. A benefit check was given to 61 people from amongst those referred to the area team over a period of a month:

> This project showed that there was low take-up of benefits among people who made contact with a social services area team; two-thirds of the people we saw seemed not to be claiming all the benefits to which they were entitled...A total of £3591 in lump sums and £8382 per annum in weekly benefit has been gained so far as a result of the project.   (Cohen and Tarpey, 1982, p.3)

It is worth making the point that adequate diagnostic ability is important not only to ensure that problems are not missed, but also to ensure that wrong advice is not given, perhaps as a side-effect of some other objective. Smith, for example, describes the disruption of a supportive relationship between and elderly disabled man and a middle-aged disabled woman. A social worker (well-meaning but lacking training in welfare rights) got them to move in together, not recognising the perils of the cohabitation rule: 'Three local tribunals, one precedent-setting High Court case, one decided Commissioners' case and one pending Commissioners' case later, Mrs Robinson has finally solved the problem of withdrawal of her independent income. She has got the pensioner shipped out into a sheltered flat' (Smith, 1982, p.15).

The question of adequate identification and diagnosis of problems also bothers Becker, MacPherson and Silburn, in relation to their findings as to the types of supplementary benefit case which social workers found 'most difficult'. Some of these were as expected: delays (25 per cent of respondents); single payments (21 per cent). But others ranked surprisingly low: additional requirements (8 per cent); cohabitation (5 per cent); fraud (2 per cent). The authors are unconvinced, suspecting that a lack of understanding of, rather than a low occurrence of problems in these areas was involved: 'Many social workers state that they have not got the knowledge they need to be able to advise adequately.

They argue that they are caught in [a]...complex benefits jungle...the individual social worker is often powerless, through lack of knowledge, to know what to do next' (Becker, MacPherson and Silburn, 1983, pp.26 – 30).

We thus have a situation in which project after project reveals undiagnosed failure to claim benefits within social work settings; there is clear evidence of the (unmet) need for social workers to have at least minimum standards of welfare rights knowledge; and it is clear that even this minimum requires a fairly good level of awareness of the subject.

How far along the advocacy scale?

There are a number of tangled themes contained within the above illustrations. First: in what does the case for welfare rights within social work lie? At least four possibilities have emerged :

(1) a minimum, albeit substantial, knowledge is essential to permit even the identification of problems;
(2) as (1), but with the rider that this minimum cannot be achieved without the experience that is derived from a more active welfare rights role;
(3) welfare rights work gives credibility to the social worker's contribution in other aspects of his or her role;
(4) implicit in a number of the comments made by welfare rights enthusiasts has been a belief that welfare rights is so important to the client's well-being that an *active* role must, by definition, be a part of social work. This is tied up with the notion of the pervasive influence of poverty; and of welfare rights as a preventive as well as a remedial strategy.

This brings us to the second point concerning the above action research evidence: who was responsible for how much action? Examples included social workers conducting the take-up work; rights workers conducting it within social services settings; social and rights workers together; and other types of staff in various combinations. As it is social workers with whom we are mainly concerned in this chapter, we must ask, then, if it is enough for them to identify problems and refer the client elsewhere for further action; or should the social worker be 'out front' with the calculator and letter of appeal? And how far should the social worker follow up a case? To a tribunal hearing? To the Social Security Commissioners? At what point, if at all, is it right to hand a case on to somebody else? And how far should *issues* be taken up, when they are raised by individual cases? That is, should social workers be responsible for 'cause' as well as 'case' advocacy; and if so, to what extent?

The conceptualisation of advice and advocacy as a spectrum of action, with relatively passive advice-giving at one extreme, ranging through a variety of forms of intervention – negotiation, representation – into 'cause advocacy' and action for wider change at the other extreme, is essential to a clear presentation of the debate. Bull (1980, especially pp.70 – 77) has developed this idea of an 'advocacy continuum' in some detail, describing '...a continuum of activity, along which different actors will travel, with different goals and with different levels of awareness'. It may be argued that social workers should not be on the continuum at all, that it is acceptable or even desirable for some or even all social workers to have nothing whatsoever to do with welfare rights. I do not accept such arguments, as will be apparent from my emphasis above on minimum standards. Once one accepts the necessity for minimum standards, which by definition must require some degree of informed advice-giving, then the question is not one of whether or not the social worker should be on the continuum, but of how far along it he or she should progress.

It is possible for those who are themselves champions of the welfare rights cause to take, nevertheless, a fairly 'non-prescriptive' approach to the question of the role of social workers. In 1982, Nathan Goldberg, the then editor of *Social Work Today,* suggested that I should act as commissioning editor for a special three-issue series focusing on social security problems. It would be concerned more with theoretical questions than with the day-to-day cut and thrust of the 'Benefits' column, which I was at that time also editing; and we decided that one of the three issues of the journal would focus on the question of welfare rights and social work. My first instinct was to set up a gladiatorial contest between pro-welfare rights and anti-welfare rights factions; but it then occurred to me that it would be less obvious, and perhaps more constructive, to juxtapose instead the views of those who insisted strongly on the social worker's welfare rights role and those who, while in the rights-promoting business themselves, nevertheless took a more permissive stance. In the 'prescriptive' corner, then, was Roger Smith, while the 'non-prescriptive' position was set out by David Bull. Both are supporters and promoters of welfare rights activity, but with rather different emphases where social workers are concerned.

In his contribution, Bull (1982b) questions the assumption that social workers *should* have an advocacy role, any more than teachers or doctors. I would argue (without wishing to underestimate either the potential for welfare rights work with the teaching or medical professions, or the links between poverty and education and health issues) that the answer to this question lies at least partly in the more specific and structured type of intervention of teachers and doctors, who have more clearly delimited goals and operate frequently in a very specialised setting – the classroom, the surgery. Another part of the answer lies in the more obvious and intimate involvement of social work with poverty. Bull goes on to argue, though, that even if we accept that

> advocacy is *inherent* in the social work task in a way that is lacking from the obligations of other helping professionals...need it follow that it is the responsibility of *each and every social worker?* Or can individual social workers legitimately argue that they lack the necessary skills and/or temperament?

He follows up this question by considering how far the social work profession has taken a collective view; whether it has taken the step of 'arrogating to itself an advocacy role that is binding on its members'. In fact, his investigations find BASW (unlike its United States counterpart, which specifically embraces advocacy) to be vague and ambivalent. He does, though, find a good deal of significance in a phrase from BASW's 1975 *Code of Ethics*: 'each member of the Association undertakes that, to the best of his ability...he acknowledges a responsibility to help clients to obtain all those services and rights to which they are entitled' (British Association of Social Workers, 1975, para. 10).

> What does it mean, though [asks Bull] for the social worker to act 'to the best of his ability': is he obliged to maximise his ability; or is he entitled to plead below-average ability in *some* social work roles?. . .the latter, non-prescriptive view. . .is the only possible position that we can adopt if we accept what are surely truisms: we are not all equally capable of acquiring every skill that our jobs may from time to time demand; and. . .not all social workers are temperamentally inclined for this (or for many another) task. . .
> I hope to continue. . .to do my modest bit towards increasing the ability of *interested* social workers to be advocates for their clients. To expect a universally enthusiastic response to my efforts, and to those of like-minded colleagues, would entail, however, a degree of pretension to which I must decline to aspire. (Bull, 1982b, pp.12–13)

This is too pluralistic a stance for Smith. After a forceful presentation of the advantages of welfare rights skills in social work, and some of the pitfalls entailed in their absence, he concludes that: 'The argument is that social workers must know about the benefit situation of their clients. It is not within the purview of a social worker to decide on an individualistic assessment of his or her own interests and aptitudes.' It is interesting to note, though, that Smith does not see his proposals as a particularly adventurous sally forth along the advocacy continuum. He, in similar terms to my argument above, is after minimum standards. Recognising the importance of context (to which I shall return below) he adds that:

> the varying nature of the alternative or supportive welfare rights available to a social worker will affect the part the latter has to play in the provision of welfare rights advice and advocacy. So will the particular nature of his or her clients. What can we say is the minimum amount of welfare rights knowledge required of a social worker practising in a local authority area team? It is :
>
> — Sufficient knowledge of welfare benefit schemes and the problems attendant on low incomes to allow an understanding of their impact on individuals;

— Sufficient diagnostic ability and knowledge in relation to benefits and tax to be able to 'smell a rat' when something is wrong or to detect possibly unclaimed benefit. (Smith, 1982, p.15)

My own view is that, given certain conditions, there is scope, as Bull suggests, for individual social workers to choose the speed and braking power with which they proceed along the advocacy continuum. These conditions are that :

(i)   minimum standards are observed;
(ii) a suitably detailed assessment has been undertaken of available alternative sources of advice and advocacy and adequate referral procedures established;
(iii) the agency has developed a clear policy concerning (i) and (ii) and that any exercise of individual discretion by a social worker as to degree of involvement in welfare rights, takes place within the framework of such a policy.

The context is indeed important. It is no use referring on to other agencies unless such alternative sources of help actually exist at an adequate level. If they do not, serious consideration must be given to the implications for local policies in relation to advice service provision, social work practice, or both. It is also true that individual social workers, teams or units with a specialist focus (a specialised client group such as disabled people) or a particular role (intake rather than long term) will have different needs in relation to welfare rights, which could be catered for by different information or training packages and different referral practices.

If the above is accepted, then the way forward for this debate in the future will be to consider such problems as how to identify what is a reasonable approach to minimum standards of welfare rights knowledge; how to develop adequate local advice networks (of which more in Chapter 3); and how to develop referral systems which actually work (further discussed in Chapter 5).

Signs of change

If new pressures and expectations are building up which will draw social work closer to welfare rights, then we should expect to see some signs that this is beginning to feed through into social work practice. There are signs, I think, that new approaches to benefit problems are taking hold within some SSDs. The idea of the 'benefit check' is one approach which could spread and prove to be of major significance. As far as I am aware, the most systematic application of this has been undertaken by Strathclyde Social Work Department, which has sought to incorporate benefits 'screening' into normal social work procedures. A 'benefits check' is being introduced as part of standard intake interview procedures, and will also cover certain long-term clients and cases where cash assistance is being considered under section 12 of the Social Work (Scotland) Act 1968. The 'benefits check' has been piloted in a systematically increasing number of area teams in Strathclyde from January 1984 (Oliver, 1984).

This system is similar to Cohen and Rushton's proposal for a 'general financial assessment':

> we recommend that it is offered even to clients who have not come with a welfare rights problem. Social workers can often be instrumental in improving their clients' take-up of benefits and services, but where clients do not present specific rights problems they sometimes slip through the net... a social worker may miss possible entitlements if she does not carry out a systematic financial assessment. Every social worker should therefore make it a rule to check thoroughly the financial position of every client who is on a low wage or living on state benefits, if [the client] agrees. (Cohen and Rushton, 1982, p.28)

Discussing their work in Islington, Cohen and Tarpey (1982, p.25) report that:

> we hope to work on ways of integrating welfare rights with the rest of social services work, so it can be done with the minimum of effort and the maximum results. We are thinking of adding benefit checks to existing social services routines; as in Lambeth, where home help organisers assess people's need for attendance allowance and other benefits when they assess their need for a home help, or in Islington's Finsbury team, where social

workers are given benefit information to check when they assess someone for registration as disabled.

Where a SSD goes systematically down this road, an interesting question will arise as to the relationship between the SSD area office function and the advice centre-type function. Certainly, social work offices will be doing lots of things which advice centres do not, notably as regards their statutory functions. But how far will the SSD area office have become, additionally, an advice centre? There are undoubtedly firm supporters of SSDs' involvement in the advice business. As Tony Bennett (1984a) puts it : 'I think social services departments could greatly enhance their reputation – and also become more aware of need in the community – were they to move onto the high street and offer advice on benefits and rights'.

There is, though, a difference between the SSD's setting up a separate advice centre, with an 'image' distinct from that of social work office, and the SSD social work offices themselves taking on greater advice functions. The very fact that social workers, as noted above, have statutory 'controlling' funtions in relation to child care and mental health, is bound to deter certain claimants who would regard the association as stigmatising. For example, in 1983, *Social Work Today* (news item, 18 October 1983, p.4), covering a BASW study day on social services and the unemployed, reported on Jennie Popay's presentation of some results from a survey of redundant car factory workers in Strathclyde. Seventy per cent of the sample did not know where their social work office was; many did not know what services it provided; and a third of the sample said 'they would not approach the department even if they had a problem, in some cases because of the stigma attached to such contact'.

It is for such reasons that I argued above that, while those who do call upon SSDs for help should expect a service in relation to benefit advice at least up to the necessary minimum standards, nevertheless social work offices cannot be regarded as substitutes for advice centres.

It is, of course, not possible to extend the role of any group of workers without considering the necessary support facilities and working time. Welfare rights work is time-consuming and social workers are generally not sitting around in their offices looking for something else to do. Where is the time to come from? Various combinations of the following factors may apply.

(i)   Social workers already spend a lot of time on benefit-related work. This could be done much more swiftly, given better training, information and streamlined procedures.
(ii) The 'preventive' value of welfare rights work will feed through in reducing the need for other kinds of intervention in a number of cases.
(iii) Some re-ordering of priorities may be necessary.
(iv) Additional staff may be required.

These considerations clearly indicate the need for welfare rights work in social services to be a matter of conscious policy and not of unconscious drift.

I shall now go on to consider the question of the supportive resources which social workers should have if their welfare rights intervention is to be effective; and the relationship which this question of support may have to that of enthusiasm for the task.

Support for the social worker

I began this chapter by doubting the stereotype of the social worker as a 'psychologically-inclined avoider of material problems' and speculated that a quite different picture might emerge, given appropriate agency priorities and back-up resources. I would like to explore this question a little further.

Parsloe and Stevenson's finding (1978), in their study of the 'practitioner's view', that almost all social workers interviewed had to deal with financial problems while only about a third of them actually liked this aspect of the work, is widely quoted. There is other evidence to suggest that the 'anti-material' stereotype is not entirely without foundation. For example, Jo Campling, outlining her and Brian Bridge's 1977 study of local authority social workers' approaches to clients' employment problems (Bridge and Campling, 1978) illustrates from interviewees' responses some attitudes which are not encouraging:

> the majority, despite unemployment figures in their areas, were inclined to view the problem as one of individual pathology. It was an emotional and psychological problem, linked to the general inadequacy of the client, often the unemployment element being seen as symptomatic of some other personal problem to be dealt with.
>
> One extreme view was expressed thus : 'We have to distinguish between problems and symptoms of problems, as with many kinds of deprivation. It is important not to overemphasise the job side. Social workers should concentrate on the individual. The same cause which prevents the client from getting a job also prevents the forming of lasting relationships. Unemployment is a cop out for problems within the individual.' (Campling, 1980, p.12)

It is not my purpose here to stray too far beyond my objective of focusing on welfare rights, rather than on related phenomena such as unemployment: however, it is clear that the arguments concerning undue emphasis on the psychological, at the expense of the material, apply in other areas apart from that of shortage of money as such.

Holman, on the other hand, has seen welfare rights as potentially reconciling the 'traditional' social work versus anti-poverty work dilemma. Observing that social workers have been criticised 'for diagnosing emotional needs where the real need was material and [for] failing to work for political changes in order to combat poverty', he argues that: 'Their dilemma...has contributed to the rise of welfare rights activity in the late 1960s and the 1970s. For in welfare rights can be found a means of providing clients with more money and yet retaining the individualised relationship' (Holman, 1973, p.358). He is, of course, referring here to the 'near end' of the advocacy continuum.

All of the above elements are no doubt present. However, my money for the best bet in terms of making progress is on Cohen and Tarpey's interpretation (1982, p.26) of the position:

> social workers' frustration in dealing with welfare rights could

be reduced if they were given adequate welfare rights training and information. Without this training, their main experience of welfare rights is its most infuriating aspect : endless telephone calls, chasing up lost or late DHSS payments or sorting out other problems caused by DHSS maladministration. They often do not have the knowledge to go beyond the immediate problem of the lost giro and, for example, check someone's benefit in detail to ensure that they are getting everything they can. This kind of welfare rights work provides much more job satisfaction, for example, working out that DHSS owes someone arrears of benefit and helping them claim it, or encouraging someone through a successful attendance allowance claim. If social workers were more often involved with the more detailed kind of welfare rights work, they would find it more satisfying and feel they were achieving more concrete results.

What back-up resources are, then, required? Clear agency policy and corresponding management objectives are essential in setting the overall scene. Information systems and training programmes are discussed in Chapters 5 and 6 respectively. But systems and programmes will not look after themselves; and neither support from policy-makers, nor sympathetic management, nor enthusiasm from social workers, will stand much chance of holding the overall system together without some sort of co-ordinating resource unit, certainly if the agency is at all large. Calls for such resources have been made in the past. For example, Chris Melotte, whose findings are quoted in more detail in Chapters 5 and 6, concluded from an interview survey of 86 social workers in 1976, that SSDs should appoint 'at least one specialist officer for welfare benefits who would be responsible for: the information system...providing advice and expertise to fieldwork staff...recommending and pressing for administrative reforms in the interest of welfare claimants' (Melotte, 1977, p.17).

As a member of CPAG's National Executive Committee, I was closely involved in the formulation of the Group's proposal for a 'welfare rights resource', the case for which is argued vigorously by Smith in the CPAG submission to Barclay. It is therefore not surprising that I should firmly endorse the CPAG position that, in the words of that document:

> Every SSD should fund a welfare rights resource. The functions
> of such a resource would be:
>
> (a) to provide specialist advice to SSD staff;
> (b) to assist in the more complex cases;
> (c) to establish and maintain adequate information research
>   systems;
> (d) to provide in-service training (via induction, refresher and
>   specialist courses). (Smith, 1981, p.19)

In the next chapter, I shall consider the options for providing
such a resource, with a particular (but not exclusive) focus on
the concept of the local authority welfare rights service.

3

A Welfare Rights Resource: The Main Options and the Local Authority Role

The importance of establishing a local and accessible welfare rights resource for social services agencies is a central theme of this book. The possibilities considered in subsequent chapters – in terms of training, information systems and action on wider issues – are all considerably enhanced if an effective welfare rights resource is there to play a supportive and enabling role.

The most effective approach to this will often be 'in-house' provision. It is also possible to make arrangements with outside agencies – a local advice centre, or perhaps an academic institution – and this is an option which should be seriously considered, depending on the type and scale of such provision which exists (or could exist, with a bit more funding) locally.

Some agencies make use of welfare rights resources which are available nationally, rather than locally. For example, one of the various types of subscription which may be taken out to CPAG includes not only special access to a telephone advisory service, but also opportunities to attend seminars on detailed aspects of problem areas of benefits. However, this is best seen as a supplement to, rather than a substitute for, the sort of readily-available *local* resource which will be needed to provide effective back-up to social services staff.

However successfully links with an 'outside' local resource may be established in some areas, it is nevertheless likely that larger organisations will lean towards an 'in-house' arrangement, perhaps partly out of habit, but principally to avoid the organisational and communication difficulties which an outside arrangement may entail. Local authorities (LAs) are likely to look to internal resources, although it should be noted that this does not necessarily mean that a welfare rights service will be located within the SSD itself : LA welfare rights units now often have a much wider remit than the servicing of the SSD, even if they are located within that department, and a significant minority are located elsewhere, perhaps in the chief executive's, town clerk's or housing department. (In such cases, it would be interesting to know how far real or potential communication difficulties in practice approach the scale of those which might apply where an outside agency is concerned.)

The larger voluntary sector agencies may also want to consider an in-house arrangement; as may other social services agencies such as the probation service – for example, the West Yorkshire Probation Service has done pioneering work in this respect (Lancaster, 1984). In all cases, a welfare rights resource located in a larger agency may well prove able to support, to one degree or another, smaller local organisations which lack the resources to make their own provision.

Before proceeding to look in more detail at the various options, it is as well to remind ourselves that the welfare rights resource will be seeking to provide relevant support not only to social workers, but also to other groups of social services workers (as well as possibly a wider range of 'customers', depending on its remit).

I shall now further consider some of the issues involved in 'plugging in' to an outside body as a welfare rights resource.

Using an outside resource

A great deal depends here on the particular local situation. If, for example, a substantial advice centre is present in the locality, it may be a pointless duplication of effort and resources to set up a separate welfare rights unit for the purpose of servicing social services staff. Similarly, it may be more productive to spend a given amount of money on funding the upgrading of an existing local agency, rather than devote a greater amount to setting up a completely new unit.

Moreover, if management in the particular social services agency tends to be over-cautious and is unlikely to cope well with its own welfare rights unit, it may be sensible to subscribe to an outside body to take advantage of the flexibility which such 'independence' can provide. For example, if the welfare rights unit is to take its own cases direct, as well as advise social services staff, a manager who is afraid to 'upset the DHSS' might see attractions in acquiring the expertise of an outside advice body, while avoiding any conflict which might arise from vigorous specialist welfare rights casework. Such calculations are likely to prove forlorn, of course, as better-informed social workers are likely to step up the tempo of their own advocacy (which, as I argued in Chapter 2, will not necessarily be unwelcome to the DHSS) : but it is nevertheless a fact that managers who, rightly or wrongly, regard welfare rights as a little radical for their taste, may even so recognise the need for such expertise and wish their agency to flirt without marrying it.

Alternatively, managers who, made of sterner stuff, are actively enthusiastic about welfare rights work, may nevertheless see advantages in keeping the welfare rights resource itself outside of the agency – perhaps as a tactical move concerning advocacy directed against their own organisations. For example, a manager in the SSD may encourage his staff to represent clients in dispute with the DHSS (hence the need for welfare rights skills) but, in areas where it is part of the same LA, may not wish them to tangle with the housing department (hence the advantages of an 'outside' unit). This question of 'independence' is discussed further below.

There are also, though, real pitfalls which can arise in using an outside agency. They can be overcome with thought and care, but need to be clearly identified.

The first consideration is to be sure that the outside body does, in fact, have the resources to do the job, even taking into account whatever subscription fee or other funding arrangement is agreed. A financially hard-pressed advice centre, on the alert for fund-raising possibilities, may offer more than it can deliver, achieving little more than an enhancement of its own cash flow – which may be highly desirable in itself, but which hardly serves our purposes here. Subscribing agencies should satisfy themselves that a realistic assessment of resources, and not merely faith, hope and over-optimism, lies behind any agreement which is reached.

As noted above, communication is also a key consideration. There must be regular meetings to assess and plan progress, involving staff at all appropriate levels and locations in both agencies; good postal and telephone contacts; and a clear understanding of the respective roles and objectives of each organisation. Such considerations as these are, of course, far from unknown in relation to different parts of the same agency, so they certainly need not be seen as decisive obstacles to the use of an outside resource ; but the extra organisational distance does call for extra care.

What sort of agency might prove to be appropriate to this sort of role? A good local advice centre is the obvious possibility. I have also referred to the potential involvement of an academic instiution : some universities, polytechnics and colleges have departments with a tradition of interest in poverty issues and they should certainly be well-placed to look after the training side of the resource role. There are, though, various other possibilities. Holman, in the early 1970s, cited lack of co-operation, or even obstructiveness, by SSD management as grounds for arguing that 'in each local authority is needed a welfare rights agency, quite independent of the Council, which would advocate for any cases referred by social workers'. It would also have wider advice functions, would seek to 'identify matters of welfare rights policy' and would provide social workers with 'up-to-date knowledge and particular expertise with special cases'. Although one hopes that obstructiveness on the part of management is nowadays less of an issue, the question of 'independence' is important and is a significant theme of this chapter. For the moment, though, it is interesting to note Holman's point (1973, p.362) concerning the possible role of BASW:

> It seems generally assumed that such welfare rights agencies should function under the auspices of the CPAG. Consideration should also be given to them being sponsored by the BASW. If

the social work profession believes that welfare rights is a legitimate professional activity, it seems reasonable that it should both provide the facilities through which it can be practised and be prepared to protect members from employers who discourage its application.

Wendy Hayward, Angela Julia and Penny Morgan (1977) have described an arrangement whereby a part-time 'citizens' rights officer' was seconded to Kingston SSD from the local citizens' advice bureau (CAB). The role of this officer was to

establish close working relationships with social workers, organise all the material on citizens' rights, using the resources available to CABs and act as a link between the department and the CAB network...her role may be summarised as advising staff and their clients about rights and entitlements and assisting clients to obtain their rights, adopting an advocacy role where necessary and appropriate.

There are no doubt a number of possible variants on related themes. A note of caution must be sounded, though, as regards the sometimes-canvassed idea of the DHSS itself functioning as a welfare rights resource for social services agencies. The issues here are just the same as those, discussed in Chapter 2, which surround the question of the DHSS's 'doing welfare rights' directly for clients : one party to a dispute, actual or potential, cannot provide independent advice to the other party. Nevertheless, some experiments along these lines have been conducted. Reporting on the secondment of two DHSS officers to Essex SSD, as part of 'a year long project to improve knowledge about people's rights to welfare benefits', *Social Work Today* (18 October 1983, p.24) has decribed an initiative whereby : 'What benefits are available and to whom, will be the subject of a series of seminars in each area of the county council. These will be attended by field social workers, staff in residential homes, home helps, probation officers and other relevant professions.'

Wirral SSD and the Birkenhead DHSS office were early explorers of this sort of arrangement. Commenting on a six-month secondment of a DHSS officer to the SSD, the Director of Social Services disconcertingly, but no doubt accurately, observed that 'the majority of clients coming to our department are not getting their full entitlement'. The DHSS officer concerned took the view that 'anyone whose work involves dealing with people who are possible claimants should have a good working knowledge of benefits – not just social workers but also home helps, day and residential care staff and health visitors'. Her role seems to have consisted of a vigorous programme of talks to a wide range of groups, with follow-up via individual advice, plus acting as 'resident expert' for SSD staff (news item, *Community Care*, 18 November 1982).

I would in no way seek to diminish the useful contribution which these officers will have made. Given their purpose and position in operating a fairly well-publicised DHSS initiative, they will no doubt have had the time and training to avoid the pitfalls which would be involved in approaching an understaffed DHSS local office for accurate advice, so my reservations have nothing to do with factual reliability of the general benefit information. Rather it is a question of interpretation of contentious points and the achievement of an unqualified pro-client approach to advocacy : with the best will in the world, this is not appropriately provided by the 'other side'.

I shall turn now to the in-house welfare rights resource, and in particular, the LA welfare rights service. It is interesting to consider such services not just as resources for social services staff, but also as innovations in which SSDs have often played a major role.

The local authority welfare rights service

The early stirrings of LA welfare rights initiatives can be traced to the late 1960s. Activity at this time was indeed modest: for example, writing about representation at supplementary benefit appeal tribunals, Tony Lynes (1970, p.125) observed that 'The Child Poverty Action Group and a handful of social workers and others have provided skilled representation in a very small number of cases'. In the same volume (a collection of Fabian essays) David Bull described the mixed success of CPAG's dealings with Manchester LA in encouraging benefit take-up efforts, observing that 'the enthusiasm of a few councillors and officials cannot jolt a whole bureaucracy into innovation' (Bull, 1970, p.140). It was Manchester, though, which subsequently appointed the first welfare rights officer as such, in 1972. However, the first LA welfare rights-type post seems to have been Oxfordshire Children's Department's appointment, in 1969, of former CPAG Secretary Tony Lynes to the post of 'Family Casework Organiser'. This was an already existing post, inappropriately titled for its new purpose. Lynes's role entailed acting as an adviser on benefit issues to social services staff and included the preparation of information materials such as a guide to means-tested benefits. He also undertook directly a good deal of advice-giving to claimants, negotiation with the DHSS and other appropriate bodies, and representation at appeal tribunals. As Lynes (1985) puts it, 'I suppose I would have called myself a "family finances consultant" '. This post became part-time in 1970 and lapsed when Lynes left in 1971, shortly before Manchester's initiative commenced.

These were early and fragmented developments. More consistent pressure for the appointment of WROs within SSDs began to build up in the next few years. One aspect of the accompanying debate has been described in Chapter 2 in the context of the 'self-help versus professionalism' issue. Other aspects of the pros and cons were set out in some perceptive observations by Peter Sharkey, who saw considerable advantages but also potential pitfalls in the idea:

The main justification for welfare rights activity within social service departments is on 'preventative' grounds...there is a vast amount of unmet financial need...the role of a welfare rights officer would be as a source of advice, help, or training for social workers who are venturing for the first time into these untrodden areas.

[However]: there is a danger that social workers and their seniors would have a clear conscience that the subject was being covered without there being any shift in emphasis within the department as a whole towards an advocate position on behalf of the more disadvantaged groups within the community.

[And]:Worst of all, such an innovation might reduce the impetus for change of the whole system of social security provision...an uncritical concern with publicity, information and advice to increase the 'take-up' of benefits might help to maintain the present system rather than change it. As a pressure group, the Child Poverty Action Group has faced this real dilemma...A welfare rights officer would likewise need to maintain this critical aspect if he was not to be accused of making a poor system of social security more rigid. (Sharkey, 1973, pp.391—2)

The last point, the danger of helping to perpetuate the status quo by tending to some of its most hard-hit victims, is in my experience well understood within welfare rights circles. For this reason, a continuing debate and a good deal of practical effort has been devoted towards generalising the day-to-day experiences of WROs into lessons to be translated into pressure for policy change. This no doubt reflects the close identification with the 'poverty lobby' which has characterised the new LA-based welfare rights services during the last ten or so years. This question is discussed in the context of welfare rights and social work in Chapter 7.

Sharkey's other concern, the possibility that WROs may be seen as the SSD's 'token' anti-poverty effort, thereby diverting energies away from changing attitudes and approaches elsewhere in the department, is one which has also exercised WROs in practice, and which calls for vigilance in seeking to place, and keep, anti-poverty initiatives on the agenda at every level.

One aspect of this sort of problem is the danger of 'anti-training', whereby social services staff begin to 'unload' welfare rights problems onto the WRO, to the extent that they themselves begin to know *less* about the subject than they otherwise would have done. When I began work as a WRO in 1974, I was initially located in an office immediately next door to a social work team, and at one stage myself became concerned that this process might be taking place. I countered it by making sure that I was involving the social worker, and not merely issuing a set of technical instructions. Other WROs have reported similar concerns: but Paul Burgess's reassuring view (1983) is, I think, correct, provided that the WRO consciously resists the temptation to 'take over':

> There is, of course, an argument that if welfare rights specialists are employed then the incentive for other staff to equip themselves to deal with welfare rights information is diminished. In fact, that is not my experience: provided with the means to obtain reliable information, preferably quickly, and provided with the chance to discuss the unusual case or the variations in policy which are commonplace, interested individuals make intelligent use of the specialist resource.

Burgess was in fact the appointee to the initial 1972 WRO post in Manchester referred to above (Burgess, 1973). Manchester's establishment of the first welfare rights *team* and the spread of WROs to a number of other LAs (including the creation of my own post in Newcastle upon Tyne) took place in 1974. LA welfare rights services as such thus have a history of a little over a decade, at the time of writing.

Before proceeding any further, though, with this historical account of developments, I should make three qualifying points. First, although I have used the most common term, 'welfare rights officer', some staff will be found to have different designations ('welfare rights worker'; 'welfare benefits officer'). Secondly, it is difficult to be exact on these historical aspects, as it can be hard to find out about work which is not well-publicised externally; and there are also problems of definition where, for example, a community worker has a welfare rights-type remit. Thirdly, it should be borne in mind, as noted above, that LA welfare rights services may well have wider concerns than the servicing of SSDs (they may service other departments and agencies and will frequently take their own caseloads direct) and will not necessarily be located within the SSD – although the main emphasis, certainly in the early years, has been on the social services setting.

Following the initial appointments in 1972—4, the number of LA WROs grew rapidly, so that by the end of 1976, about

25—30 authorities were employing at least one WRO and a few teams were beginning to emerge. In a 1976 study, Tony Simpson (1978, p.3) identified 32 LA welfare rights workers.

Economic difficulties and consequent constraints on LA expenditure seem to have held back development after 1976, giving rise to a fairly stable picture in the late 1970s. But ironically, these same national economic problems, notably the onset of mass unemployment, have created a renewed interest amongst LA policy-makers, in spite of the direct costs of making provision for welfare rights services. There has thus been a recent increase both in the number of LAs making provision and in the number of WROs employed by some individual LAs. At the time of writing, it has to be said that we do not have exact up-to-date knowledge of how many LAs currently employ WROs, how many they employ and how they use them. My own knowledge is based on over ten years' close involvement with LA welfare rights work and extensive contact with the network of services represented in the national Welfare Rights Officers Group. Nevertheless, how many new services are not connected to the national network is an unknown factor and there is an obvious need for further research.

In this chapter, I shall seek to draw on experience acquired in different parts of the country to summarise existing types of provision and to outline some of the main issues surrounding LA welfare rights work. In doing so, I shall generally not seek to 'endorse' a particular structure, the idea being rather to identify different approaches; but some principles likely to be of general application will be pointed out.

What is local authority welfare rights work?

The distinction should be emphasised between the LA as a benefit-administering agency, with attendant responsibilities for publicity, standards of administration and so on; and the LA as provider of welfare rights information, advice and advocacy. These two roles may well overlap: for example, a take-up campaign could be seen both as a welfare rights initiative and as good administrative practice; and, say, an LA housing department may well join forces with a welfare rights service to mount such an effort. On the other hand, the two roles may conflict: for example, a local authority WRO will frequently find it necessary to argue against an administrative decision concerning an individual rent rebate award, or indeed some aspect of the LA's overall rebate policy. More is said below concerning the management of conflict in such circumstances.

A recent and striking example of welfare rights—-administrative collaboration has been the introduction of housing benefit, which has amongst other things linked LAs more closely to the administration of the social security system. Several LA housing departments, including Glasgow, Manchester and Newcastle, have collaborated closely with welfare rights advisers. This is undoubtedly good practice, provided that it is openly recognised, not least by WROs themselves, that first loyalty on the welfare rights side should be, by definition, to the claimant in the event of any apparent conflict of interests.

LA welfare rights work is sometimes assumed to be primarily concerned with take-up of benefits, in the sense of generating claims (for an analysis which tends to stress this aspect, see Anne Howard, 1978). But in fact advocacy on problem cases figures large, as does, in some LAs, work on policy issues. Intervention can be on several levels. For example:

Advice/advocacy: providing advice services direct to the public and/or by advising less specialist advisers, such as social workers or housing staff (the knowledge gained from 'case contact' being in fact indispensable to all other aspects of welfare rights work);

'Community development'-type work: seeking to strengthen community resources, such as the capacity of, say, tenants' associations to advise their members or mount campaigns on specific issues;

Publicity: seeking to bring entitlements to the attention of potential claimants, using various methods including large-scale 'take-up' campaigns;

Training: spreading knowledge of welfare rights to a variety of audiences, ranging potentially from general talks for the public to intensive and relatively technical training for professional staff and other relevant advisers;

Policy-orientated work: seeking to influence local and/or national policy on benefits so as to secure improvements and/or limit adverse changes to the benefit system.

LAs can and do pursue various permutations of the above, depending on objectives, priorities and resources deployed. It is important to note, though, that (certainly in the modern context of mass unemployment) any kind of welfare rights activity will generate a demand – often a very large demand – for the *first* item, that is advice and advocacy. Whether or not it is intended to meet such a demand to any degree (and I would argue that some sort of 'real life' input is required, whatever the main focus) some means of dealing with it needs to be devised in advance. (The same is true to some degree of the other areas of work indicated, but they are much more easily rationed.) Many welfare rights projects have found their intended pattern of work disrupted by an overwhelming demand for individual advice and support. If resources are not available to meet such a demand, rationing (for instance, by efficient referring-on) must be planned well ahead, not practised informally and/or as a panic measure.

Before discussing different models of welfare rights service, I shall first of all summarise briefly some of the arguments in favour of, and some of those against, LA involvement in specific welfare rights provision (as distinct from the discussion in Chapter 2 of the welfare rights role of social workers) and shall focus particularly on the difficult question of 'independence'.

Why should the local authority be involved?

This question is best tackled by looking first at the positive benefits to different areas of LA responsibility.

(1) *Social services* Obviously, I need here only refer the reader to the extensive evidence presented in Chapter 2.

(2) *Housing* Some LA Housing Departments have taken an increasing interest in welfare rights in recent years, as the potential for helping tenants with rent arrears has become apparent. The advent of the new housing benefit scheme has created a greater need than ever for housing staff to be alert to a range of benefit issues.

(3) *Education* LA Education Departments are of course themselves involved in the welfare benefit field to some degree, through free school meals, clothing and various maintenance grants and so on. They will therefore have an interest in, for example, take-up campaigns. Moreover, Education Departments have an interest in ensuring that parents' and pupils' full entitlements from the main social security system are in fact secured to help avoid problems of, for example, poor diet and clothing, or a stressful home environment.

(4) *Economic development* Sustained welfare rights activity can bring into a locality large amounts of central government money, which will go to some of the most hard-pressed citizens and much of which they will spend on necessities in local shops. Thus, in the West Midlands, Strathclyde and Newcastle, LAs have to varying degrees invoked 'economic development' arguments in support of their funding of various welfare rights initiatives.

While there are thus very strong arguments in favour of LA involvement in providing welfare rights services, arguments are also sometimes advanced against. For the most part, these are similar to those put forward to oppose social workers' involvement, including the list of supposedly more appropriate channels through which the job should be done : the DHSS; computers; take-up campaigns; claimants' organisations; individual claimants themselves, and so on. These have all been discussed in Chapter 2 and I shall not repeat the arguments here. I should add to them, though, the arguments that such work should be done by social workers and/or other types of worker, such as housing staff, and not by specialist WROs; and the 'independence' argument. As regards social workers, the issues are again extensively aired in Chapter 2. As regards housing staff, insofar as substantial welfare rights work beyond potential spin-offs from housing benefit administration is intended, then the intensive nature of the work suggests that housing departments would be likely to provide for it not as an aspect of some existing post, but by appointing their own welfare rights staff – as some (Glasgow; Ipswich) have indeed done. As will become clear from my discussion of the 'independence' argument, I do not believe that housing departments provide an appropriate base for WROs.

'Independence'

In its most uncompromising form, this argument suggests that because LAs are themselves benefit-administering agencies, they cannot provide sufficiently independent welfare rights services to claimants. This is a similar argument to my own observations in relation to DHSS, so why do I not go along with the 'independence' argument as applied to LAs? As a local authority welfare rights adviser myself, I shall have to answer this question carefully, if I am to avoid charges of mere self-justification. In doing so, I should like to consider the question of 'organisational distance'; ethical aspects of welfare rights advocacy; and the myth of 'voluntary' provision.

Organisational distance

The advent, in 1982—3, of the new housing benefit system, not only extended enormously LAs' existing role in administering housing benefits, but did so in the context of widespread administrative failure, confusion and hardship (Clark, Daly and Douglas, 1984; Kemp, 1984; National Association of Citizens' Advice Bureaux, 1984). While the greater part of the blame lies at the door of Central Government, which was responsible for the fundamentally botched nature of an under-resourced scheme, LAs were nevertheless running it, and it is not surprising therefore that one of the many issues to attract attention in the aftermath of this debacle should be the independence of LA WROs in metropolitan areas (where housing and social services are part of the same tier of local government) in relation to their employers. As far as I know, this discussion is more theoretical than based on any actual incidence of failure effectively to represent claimants: it is nevertheless an important issue. Cohen (1983, p.14) puts it thus:

> The Council must...recognise that as a major benefit provider it cannot always supply impartial welfare rights advice. People must be able to get independent advice and advocacy from voluntary organisations if they are disputing the council's decision about housing benefit. There is a serious conflict of interest for any council officer, from whatever department, in advising about such disputes. Also people will not want to seek advice even from a different worker, at the same office about which they are complaining. We do not think that council plans about decentralised offices and welfare rights take account of this crucial point.

In one LA, this question of conflict of interest was raised by the chief finance officer in arguing that WROs, based in the SSD, should not represent claimants at the new housing benefit review boards. However, when the welfare rights team leader queried this proposal with a somewhat consumer-conscious Chairman of the Housing Committee, the latter is reported to have rejected such a restriction on representation with the observation that: 'This is not what I want. It is not only not what I want, it is the opposite of what I want.' The issue seems to have been successfully resolved in that LA, where WROs have since represented claimants at review boards without adverse reaction from the bureaucracy.

Although the new housing benefit scheme has generated new interest in this question, LA WROs have in fact been representing claimants in dispute with departments in the same LA for over ten years, without a significant 'independence' problem having emerged. Why is this? This is where the 'distance' between departments becomes significant. Corporate management notwithstanding, LA departments, like any other social sub-system, function to some degree as separate entities. This will obviously vary from place to place, but this effect would appear to be fairly strong in practice. In other words, an SSD-based adviser representing a claimant in dispute with the housing or education department in the same LA may not be seen by SSD management to be 'rocking the boat' any more than if the dispute was with the DHSS. In most LAs which have appointed WROs, if the latter are not based in the SSD, then they are outside the service departments altogether and based in the chief executive's department or some similarly central location. They have undoubtedly benefited from organisational distance in a way which would not be possible within a centralised structure such as the DHSS. The SSD does of course itself administer certain benefits and services, but important though these are, they are peripheral to the main income maintenance system in a way in which housing benefit certainly is not. This is why I would argue, against certain current strands of opinion, that it is unsound to locate WROs in housing departments, while location within SSDs is, and has been show by experience to be, viable (although I think Cohen's point – quoted above – concerning shared offices is sound).

Ethical aspects of welfare rights advocacy

I would suggest, though, that organisational distance is not, in itself, enough to protect the position of the LA WRO, especially when it does not apply to any significant degree, for example where the SSD-based WRO disagrees with the SSD itself, say, over a 'Section 1' payment, or an aid under the terms of the Chronically Sick and Disabled Persons legislation. An important reinforcing element here is an overt recognition by the LA, the WRO and all concerned, that the term welfare *rights* has certain ethical connotations. If a person has *rights* they cannot be conditional upon whether the body in relation to which they are to be exercised feels like bothering with them or not; or upon whether a person entrusted with advocating them feels embarrassed about doing so. Thus, the *legitimacy* of welfare rights advocacy must be recognised explicitly by the LA. This issue should be raised unambiguously at the time that policy-makers decide to set up welfare rights units, and the issue kept 'live' thereafter, to ensure that LAs and their officers at all levels are aware of the ethical implications of the sort of service which the authority has set in motion.

It is surprising how effective this can be in practice. In all my dealings, as a social services-based welfare rights adviser, with City Councillors and officers of various LA departments, including the SSD, differences of opinion on particular issues and cases have naturally arisen, and have at times been vigorously expressed, but I can recall only one instance of the right to advocate on behalf of the claimant being questioned. Moreover, there would seem to be a trend in contemporary notions of 'progressive administration' which actually welcomes some injection of 'consumer interest', of which WROs are seen to be an aspect. My own dealings with Newcastle Housing Department suggest this strongly.

Particularly important as regards the 'ethical' issue – the commitment to claimants' rights – is the role of WROs themselves in making sure that they insist on the point; and the role of councillors, who are of course responsible to the electorate for the service.

Simpson (1978, p.80) found in his survey of LA welfare rights workers, that: 'Workers in five agencies said there was conflict in relation to the workers' promotion of local authority benefits and services, such as Section 1 assistance, rate and rent rebates, etc. In this situation, the worker saw his loyalty to the claimant trying to gain access to agency provision.'

The political assumptions behind Manchester's new Housing Benefit Advisory Service also deserve note. This is a welfare rights unit in the SSD, and has wide functions : advice, advocacy, training (of LA staff, councillors and outside bodies), take-up, monitoring of service delivery and raising of policy issues. Crucially, as Peter Rush (1984, p.12) puts it, 'the HBAS is, at the insistence of the Council, independent of the Housing Benefit Office'. Such explicit political recognition of the requirements of welfare rights work is to be applauded.

Nevertheless, might not this whole issue be avoided if welfare rights services were always located within the 'non-governmental' or 'voluntary' sector?

The role of the voluntary sector

I shall place my own cards firmly on the table here. I am in favour of an arrangement whereby welfare rights services are provided in a given area by a variety of different types of agency (local authority, voluntary sector, neighbourhood projects with independent management committees) collaborating as a co-operating – not duplicating or competing – network: what the National Consumer Council (1977, p.60) has described as 'a mixed economy comprising both statutory and voluntary bodies'. More is said below of such 'advice networks'.

It follows, then, that I do not subscribe to the view that welfare rights services should be the exclusive responsibility of the voluntary sector. Certainly, such a move would cause some opportunities to be lost. 'Internal' services can offer input to policy, publicity and staff training which can be much more problematic for outside bodies – especially the policy aspect. Moreover, Anne Howard (1978, p.29) has made out an argument for the 'insider' role being useful for welfare rights casework also:

> conflict between claiment, welfare rights worker and statutory body is not necessarily discouraged in a local authority setting, as it is sometimes supposed. On the contrary, a local authority employee may be well placed to act as an intermediary between the claimant and the central and local administrators of benefits, just because he is on the local government pay roll, just because he is on the 'inside'. This may be particularly true where the welfare rights worker has a relatively free hand within usually the social services department.

Whether such 'differential access' is a desirable state of affairs is highly questionable : nevertheless, experience suggests that there is a good deal of truth in Howard's assertion.

However, I am thinking here not so much of certain advantages which might be foregone in the absence of LA services, but rather of the dubious nature of the frequent uncritical equation of the voluntary sector with 'independence'. The myth of voluntary provision is surrounded by certain conventional images : the voluntary fund-raiser waving a tin; or the imaginary hordes of caring neighbours beloved of a government anxious to stem expenditure on personal social services and shift responsibilites onto unpaid women (or 'the community', as they are sometimes known).

Some voluntary organisations are, of course, genuinely independent of government, perhaps because of a substantial public appeal income, or the support of a charitable trust, and this is all to the good. However, certainly in the advice field, provision of a service on any substantial scale is very likely to be underpinned by local authority funds; or perhaps the dubious blessing of shaky short-term funding from the Urban Aid-type programmes or the Manpower Services Commission. In a time of local authority expenditure cuts, voluntary sector funding – out on a limb, unprotected by departmental bureaucracies or effective trade union support – may well be thought to be rather less secure than 'main line' LA funding. I would argue, therefore, that there is a sense in which the greater degree of effective 'independence' is to be found at the extremes: units which have a corner to defend in mainstream LA provision; and voluntary organisations which genuinely do not rely on state funds. Between these two poles lie the various local and/or central government-funded voluntary organisations and other non-governmental bodies.

It is here that a main strength of the 'mixed economy' of advice services lies : all of the eggs are not in the one basket. On the one hand, reductions in LA funding of the voluntary sector will not smite all advice centres; on the other, neither necessarily will an adverse change of political control at the town hall. Of course, the objective of advice centres, not least in the interests of claimants, should be to ensure that none of them is smitten. They should therefore communicate, co-operate and support each other.

I shall turn now to look at various alternative possibilities for the organisation of LA welfare rights services.

Alternative structures for welfare rights

Existing welfare rights services have grown up often in a piecemeal fashion, and have reflected, organisationally and geographically, the idiosyncracies of local circumstances. Strengths and weaknesses are apparent in all of them.

It is indeed essential that a local welfare rights structure *should* reflect local circumstances and no 'ideal' model can be presented here. Nevertheless, certain general principles and dilemmas apply; and the rest of this chapter will be devoted to setting out the most important of these.

Local networks

Effective use of resources and the need for diversity both imply that direct LA welfare rights provision should be seen as part of a local network of advice centres including those in the voluntary sector and the various state-funded but semi-autonomous centres to be found in some areas. I would therefore recommend that LAs intending to make a contribution in this area should conduct or sponsor 'audits' – surveys of the nature, funding, geographical spread and so on – of existing provision, such as those which have been carried out in Birmingham (Birmingham Citizens' Advice Bureau, 1981), Cambridgeshire (Cambridgeshire Information and Advice Services Working Party, 1980), Newcastle (Fimister, 1981a) and Sheffield (Sheffield Information and Advice Services Working Party, 1980) to ensure optimal deployment of new resources (see also National Consumer Council, 1982).

The approach of some LAs has been to seek explicitly to stimulate and co-ordinate existing networks by appointing just one welfare rights adviser at a senior level with this remit (for example North Tyneside). These are recent appointments and it remains to be seen how they will develop.

Centralisation versus decentralisation

The prevalent model amongst the larger welfare rights services (Strathclyde; Manchester; Newcastle) is that of a small central unit with co-ordinating and developmental functions, acting as the 'hub' of a system of decentralised advice services (in Strathclyde, reflecting geographical size, this model is replicated in several different divisions).

Such a model has the advantage of reaching out into deprived neighbourhoods, but has two potential disadvantages (Newcastle, at least, suffers from both of them) :

(i) If there is not also a central advice centre with sufficient capacity to absorb city/town centre demand, the central unit is likely to be swamped with a demand for advice which cannot be met;
(ii) Areas lacking neighbourhood advice centres may be neglected. This problem applies in large parts of many towns and cities, and of course appears in an acute form where LAs embrace rural areas. Experiments with mobile services are relevant here, although they will inevitably suffer from problems of continuity of contact with the claimant.

Where a decentralised approach is adopted, policy-makers also need to be cautious about their use of the much-abused concept of 'neighbourhood'. Catchment areas must be realistic, every effort being made to resist the temptation to draw large, optimistic circles on maps.

There is also a question, where a decentralised system operates, of what kind of local base to use. In Manchester and Strathclyde, social work offices are used; while in Newcastle, an advice shop and community projects are preferred. Decentralised efforts need not, though, take the form of 'walk in' advice centres (although there will be a demand for these). For example, 'screening' to identify unclaimed benefits amongst day centre attenders has been developed in Strathclyde, Harlow and Newcastle alongside various other approaches. (Some of the results from Strathclyde and Harlow were described in Chapter 2.) Strathclyde and Gateshead have used mobile advice centres.

Newcastle's approach includes specialists in multiple debt problems, operating on a referral basis. Nottinghamshire provides an example of a local authority with a highly individualistic strategy deriving from the particular features and problems of the county : advisers are deployed in different localities, linking with existing resources and stimulating a wide range of welfare rights activity.

Some LAs have a sole, centrally-based WRO without decentralised 'offshoots'. As noted above, some of these (for example, North Tyneside) are specifically intended to 'plug into' existing networks; but others merely adopt the 'superhero' model, where an indefatigable WRO, centrally-based, provides policy input, training, publicity campaigns – and also does advice work and represents at tribunals. With this sort of remit, it is not possible to develop any one area of work intensively without pulling resources out of another.

Which department?

SSD: Most LA welfare rights services are based here, reflecting this department's intensive contact with poverty-related issues.

Chief Executive's/Town Clerk's: A significant minority are based here, reflecting a recognition of the inter-departmental scope for welfare rights work.

Housing: As noted above, there is a growing interest in welfare rights within housing departments. While the interest is very much to be encouraged, I have maintained above that there are strong arguments against actually locating WROs within the housing department itself. For example, Newcastle's housing department part-finances WROs whose remit is especially geared towards multiple debt problems : but the WROs are nevertheless located within the SSD, partly for the reasons described.

Consumer Protection: There should clearly be interest in

welfare rights here. There are certainly examples of funding of welfare rights-type posts within the voluntary sector deriving from this source (Avon; Tyne and Wear) although I am not aware of any direct WRO appointments.

Whichever department is chosen, it is important that appropriate inter-departmental links are cultivated.

Which committee?

The appropriate committee of the council to which the welfare rights service is responsible may simply reflect departmental location and local committee structure; but at least one LA (Sheffield) has experimented with a separate welfare rights sub-committee.

Experimental versus continuing provision

Because welfare rights is a relatively new field, projects are sometimes defined as experimental and staff appointed on temporary basis. Temporary contracts are an unsatisfactory tool in many ways, disruptive of continuity. While experimentation is of course to be encouraged, I would argue strongly that LAs should use temporary contracts only where there is some real reason to believe that provision is likely to be temporary (for example, where a 'one-off' campaign, rather than a continuing service, is specifically intended). Too frequently, it is patently obvious that the need for staff is pressing and continuing, the temporary appointment reflecting bureaucratic caution or the use of unstable sources of funding such as Urban Aid. The label 'experimental' is then used as a fig-leaf to conceal short-sighted pragmatism.

Use of 'specialisms'

In some LAs (e.g. Nottinghamshire; Newcastle) while all WROs deal with the whole field of welfare rights concern, individuals are assigned special areas of interest (for example, fuel issues; issues relating to ethnic minorities; youth unemployment) which they are expected to pursue particularly intensively. This can result in useful developmental work, although care should be taken to ensure that other staff do not then 'relax' in these subjects.

'Hybrids'

In some LAs, 'hybrid' posts have been created, such as welfare rights/social work (developed in Wandsworth, although since phased out by a 'cuts-orientated' regime); and welfare rights/community work (Sheffield). This is likely to represent special emphases in that LA, or perhaps in a particular department or office.

A variety of different approaches to the structure of welfare rights services is thus possible, and a great deal of diversity has indeed characterised the development of LA welfare rights initiatives during their short history. It is clear that SSDs have played a major role; and that SSD staff have much to gain from such services, whether or not they are actually located within that department. One element, though, which is surely common to all types of structure is the need for adequate resources, administrative and other back-up facilities, and the thinking-out of appropriate conditions of employment.

Resources and other practicalities

A number of questions need to be considered concerning the appropriate level of resources to be devoted to a given type and scale of service. It is worth setting these out, as although some of these points may seem obvious, in fact experience very definitely suggests that enthusiasm to get a new idea 'off the drawing board' can lead to certain important practicalities lagging behind other aspects of project planning.

Staffing levels

A main consideration is that it is essential to avoid *under-staffing* if objectives are to be realised. The question 'how many staff?' can be answered at two levels. First, the total numbers of staff employed : numbers range from several LAs with only one WRO, to Strathclyde with around 40. But of course one also has to take into account the extent of, and links with, other (for instance voluntary sector) provision in the area. Secondly, the number of WROs on any given welfare rights project – for example, if a busy advice centre needs two members of staff interviewing at any one time, then it will need to employ at least three, as there are many reasons why WROs will need to be working off the premises, as well as the usual provision for sickness and leave.

Salaries

Salaries constitute another important practical area. LA personnel officers, understandably anxious to keep down costs, may seek to portray the WRO as a fresh-faced young thing, primarily engaged in pressing leaflets upon cheerful claimants, and thereby justifying a grading in the more modest regions of LA scales. The reality of complex legislation, skilled negotiation and advocacy is of course somewhat different. Another version of this problem is the occasional tendency to confuse a local authority service with a claimants' self-help group: that is, 'how can you represent claimants if you are not poor yourself?' Taken to an extreme, this could be an argument for leaving all welfare rights work to self-help groups (although I have argued in Chapter 2 that the issues here are not as simple as they might at first seem). But it is not an argument for under-paying LA employees. Salaries should be reasonably comparable with those which similar staff could command elsewhere, if the service is not to suffer the discontinuities of high staff turnover.

Practical facilities

Practical facilities for interviewing, reception and waiting areas, typing, photocopying of documents and so on, are all crucial items which need to be planned in advance. There is also the essential question of the establishment and updating of information systems for the WROs' own use. These will be more expensive and voluminous than systems, such as those described in Chapter 5, which are designed for less specialist users.

Line management

Line management arrangements vary widely, reflecting local departmental structures. Some areas have fairly complex arrangements : for instance, in Strathclyde line management is separated from professional supervision which is in the hands of divisional welfare rights advisers. Where few staff are concerned, WROs generally simply 'plug in' to the departmental management structure, depending on their physical location. Some larger welfare rights services have their own internal line management structures (for example, on Tyneside, Gateshead and South Tyneside have two tiers, with senior officers; while Newcastle has three, with a principal officer responsible for policy issues and a senior responsible for day-to-day management of services).

Where there are several WROs a decision will need to be taken as to whether they should function in terms of formal organisation as a team (as at Newcastle) or, whether they should relate to diverse lines of management (as in Strathclyde).

Professional supervision and development

Professional supervision and development (which, as in the case of Strathclyde, need not lie with line management) can present problems given the highly specialised nature of the work. Where there are no other welfare rights specialists in the agency, a WRO may well be left to his or her own devices, which can be isolating. On the other hand, where there is a team, a highly creative situation can develop whereby particular officers acquire areas of special interest and expertise on which they are able to brief other welfare rights (including senior) officers. Mutual and self-education is necessary in a rapidly changing field.

There is not space here to pursue in detail these issues and others relating to relevant qualifications and experience (the need to be aware of skills from a variety of walks of life), specialist training and so on. Suffice it to say that these need to be carefully worked out beforehand. LAs thinking of moving into this area would do well to consult those with experience of operating welfare rights services: there are plenty of successes – and mistakes – from which to learn.

I trust that this chapter will have been of interest in two main respects to those concerned with the personal social services. First, the types of welfare rights service which I have described hold out the prospect of a reliable welfare rights resource which can underpin the efforts of social services agencies to equip themselves to tackle this major problem area. Secondly, here is a new field of service provision in which a number of SSDs have played pioneering roles.

I have pointed out that welfare rights services may not be situated within the SSD, or even within the LA; and they may not be concerned mainly, or even at all, with servicing social services agencies. In such cases, negotiations will need to be opened and deals struck in order to establish this essential facility. In many other cases, there will be no appropriate pre-existing service and the welfare rights resource will need to be created 'from scratch'. This is a matter of policy and resources. We turn next to the political dimension.

4

Acquiring a Welfare Rights Resource: The Political Dimension

In large numbers of local authorities up and down the country, social services staff are forced to confront the income problems of their clients without the support of a welfare rights back-up resource, or may indeed fail directly to confront such problems at least in part because of the absence of the tools to do the job.

In this chapter, I shall consider the main factors which need to be taken into account in seeking to establish a welfare rights resource. Many of the same points will apply to attempts to strengthen an existing resource, or indeed, defend one from attack, for example as a result of expenditure cuts. Moreover, while the focus of this discussion concerns the establishment of a welfare rights unit, many of the same considerations will apply to any policy innovation within social (or other) services. I have, though, neither the space nor the wish to develop an excessively theoretical or abstract analysis. My purpose will be to present the issues in concrete terms in the hope that some readers may find some of these points of direct practical application within their own local set of circumstances.

For simplicity of presentation, I shall assume that the effort in question is one to persuade the LA to set up a new unit within the SSD, although the argument may in practice concern another department or the funding of a voluntary organisation. I shall also approach the question from the hypothetical standpoint of a social services employee – say, a female social worker in a SSD area team – who has become aware of the need for such a development from her own experiences in the field. Again, there will in practice be other actors in other situations (politicians, administrators, pressure groups) who will be taking the lead, and they will perceive the issues discussed here from their own particular perspectives.

A few words concerning the processes of local government policy-making would be appropriate here. I do not propose to attempt to condense a comprehensive account of the theory and practice of local government into a couple of paragraphs, so I run the risk of over-simplification. Moreover, many readers will already be familiar with local authority political and bureaucratic policy-formulating processes through first hand experience. Nevertheless, a reminder of the nature of the policy-making context would no doubt be helpful to an analysis of how our hypothetical social worker should proceed. The process of interplay of different political elements and vested interests will occur (in varying forms) at any level of government, but it is the LA context with which we are concerned here.

The formal notion, in its simplest and least realistic form, is of course that electors elect councillors, whose policies are then relayed to officers, who carry them out. But in reality, patterns of decision-taking are far more complex, as policies are filtered through the many different layers and groupings of interests which exist within and between different political parties and council committees, and within the bureaucracy. For example, apart from party differences, there may be differences of perspective on a common issue – say, homelessness – between committees; there may be different factions within the same party on the same committee; and the extent to which a particular party group on a local council feels obliged always to pursue local party policy will also vary. These multifarious elements in turn interact with the bureaucracy: the relationships between elected councillors and local government officers at all levels are complex, subtle and varied. Who exactly is likely to influence whom and to what extent will vary between departments and between LAs. The powerful chairperson who ensures that the bureaucracy toes the party line and the weak chairperson who does exactly as the chief officer wishes, are each stereotypes at either end of a spectrum. In between lie the many different real-life patterns of political/bureaucratic relationships.

This network of interacting interests and relationships will determine, in a given LA area, the likely receptiveness of local government both to ideas originating within 'the system', and to the overtures of 'outside' bodies such as pressure groups of one sort or another. All of this has considerable implications as to where it would be most fruitful for our social worker to focus her efforts if she is successfully to 'sell' the idea of a welfare rights service.

I shall begin by considering the roles of the different interest groups which are likely to be involved – political parties; councillors; professional bodies; voluntary organisations and pressure groups; trade unions; senior LA management and other vested interests within the LA bureaucracy. I shall then go on to present briefly some real-life case examples, which illustrate some of these forces at play.

The political parties

The Labour Party

In terms of setting up welfare rights services, Labour councils seem to have a near-monopoly. Simpson (1978, p.29), referring obliquely to the Labour Party, reported that '18 of the 22 authorities in our study were of one political persuasion at the time when appointments were made'. This trend has continued in the subsequent pattern of appointments. There are various reasons for this. Welfare rights services are established as a response to poverty, and Labour Councils perceive themselves as acting in the interests of a section of their traditional constituency in making such provision. Moreover, some of the most acute and obvious manifestations of poverty are within the inner cities, where the Labour Party is likely to be politically strong. Even in other areas, where the Labour Party is not in control of the council, such has been the identification of some party branches with the welfare rights approach, that in at least one instance – in Brighton – the local Labour Party has itself initiated a major take-up campaign without LA involvement, drawing in other sympathetic local groups (Brighton Welfare Rights Campaign, 1982). A one-off campaign is a much more limited enterprise than a continuing service, but for an opposition party it is an impressive achievement.

A further factor which has become important since the 1979 General Election has been the perception within a number of Labour Councils of welfare rights as a vehicle for bolstering local resistance to what are seen as the hostile social and economic policies of central government. This has been particularly prominent in Strathclyde (see below) but one senses its presence in other areas also – Newcastle and the Greater London Council are examples.

This is not to say that the Labour Party can be regarded as the untarnished champion of welfare rights. In many areas, inaction and indifference still prevail even where high levels of social deprivation cry out for welfare rights intervention. Moreover, where services have been established, a number are arguably under-resourced in relation to the tasks which they are expected to perform, so there is still plenty of scope for lobbying in Labour-controlled territory.

The Conservative Party

Instances of Conservative Councils establishing welfare rights services appear to be rare. This will again partly reflect the social make-up of party support, and partly the related question of geographical spread of political control (the problems of hidden poverty, notably amongst the elderly, in the genteel suburbs, and of rural poverty, are very real, but do not have the high political profile of the inner cities). There will also be ideological elements, linked to the mistrust of the encouragement of rights-consciousness amongst the 'undeserving', and to related 'anti-scrounger' notions. Moreover, while the current crisis of LA expenditure will weigh against the introduction of new services anywhere, this effect is bound to be heightened where the Council has an ideological, as distinct from merely pragmatic, commitment to spending restrictions.

However, it cannot be assumed that Conservative councillors will necessarily be unsympathetic. Well-publicised cash gains for claimants can be seen as solid, non-ephemeral 'value for money' which may appeal to some aspects of Conservative thought; as may the argument – summarised later in this chapter – that welfare rights work can offset other costs. The 'economic development' aspect of welfare rights (that is, the injection of much-needed spending power into local economies to the advantage of, for example, small shopkeepers in areas of high unemployment) should also strike a chord amongst Conservatives. Further, an acceptance of wider means-testing in social security may be accompanied by a corresponding acceptance that this will exacerbate the take-up problem and thereby call for more attention to be paid to information services. Thus, in Newcastle, although the Welfare Rights Service was set up and developed by the majority Labour Party, the Conservatives, for a mixture of the above reasons, have increasingly, if cautiously, accepted the validity of its role. What is likely to happen in marginal authorities subject to changes of political control, is not clear. For the reasons given above, it should not automatically be assumed that the 'Wandsworth effect' (where one of the pioneering LA services was phased out following a change of control from Labour to Conservative) is inevitable. Even there, some provision was subsequently restored, and there are other occasional examples which are encouraging, the foremost being that of Lothian Regional Council, where a minimal service (one WRO) was considerably expanded in 1984, with all-party support, the Conservatives being the largest party (Hannah, 1985).

Research is needed to identify the circumstances in which, and the reasons for which, Conservative councillors sometimes support welfare rights initiatives. The predominant identification of LA welfare rights with Labour councils may be good for the image of the latter, but is not so good for the poor in other areas.

The Liberal—Social Democratic Party Alliance

There is not a great deal of information to go on as regards the Alliance. The former Liberal regime in Liverpool provides one, rather curious, example. That city's high levels of economic and social deprivation present a pressing need for welfare rights provision, and indeed a tradition of voluntary sector activity dates back to the 1960s (see for example, Bull, 1970; Check! Rights Centre, 1977). But the City Council's attitude both to direct provision and to support of the voluntary sector left much to be desired. One officer told Howard Sharron in 1982 that: 'Welfare rights is not looked upon as the responsibility of the local authority...the voluntary sector is more adapted to respond and we give them money to do it.' Funding a voluntary sector agency is of course a perfectly acceptable alternative : but Sharron's investigations (for *Social Work Today*) did not paint an encouraging picture here either. He found the Liverpool Welfare Rights Resource Centre – an outspoken, campaigning advice centre – to be faced with the termination of its Urban Aid funding; while more 'respectable' voluntary bodies were also in difficulties: '...the Liverpool Personal Social Services Council and the Citizens' Advice Bureaux are believed to be running into debt and cutting back because of reduction in their grants'. Social workers' welfare rights efforts, moreover, were being affected both by their own vacant posts and by the shortage of specialist advice : 'Social workers in Liverpool believe the overall effect of Liberal policies has been actually to decrease the amount of welfare rights work done in the department.' One informant told him that:

welfare rights had always been considered as part of the job and social workers used to attend tribunals on behalf of clients. However, the freezing of posts meant that social workers were being forced to concentrate on statutory work and were now turning away people looking for benefits advice...without the help of specialists, social workers were becoming less and less confident about dealing with welfare rights, and were finding it impossible to keep up with the changes. (Sharron, 1982, p.10)

The Liverpool Welfare Rights Resource Centre itself was in no doubt about the Council's approach to voluntary sector funding:

We're being closed down because we fight for people's rights! As a Centre we've fought for the rights for our clients against the DHSS, fuel boards, employers, the Council, whoever. As workers in the voluntary sector we're active trade unionists who've been resisting cuts in community groups. It seems that some councillors can't take the idea of independent bodies that stand up for local people. (Liverpool Welfare Rights Resource Centre, 1982)

This clash seems surprising on the face of it. One would expect welfare rights to accord fairly easily with Liberal notions of civil liberties and anti-corporatism. The antipathy of the Resource Centre towards the Council's overall policies of social expenditure restraint could be seen as analogous to the conflict between some Labour councils and local Community Development Projects in earlier years, rather than as indicating some inherent incompatibility between Liberals and the welfare rights approach. Nevertheless, it has to be said that Sharron's findings do suggest a more general lack of interest in welfare rights provision. Perhaps we should regard this as a local aberration not typical of Liberal attitudes elsewhere: certainly, I have found the modest Liberal presence on Newcastle City Council to be readily supportive of welfare rights initiatives. As regards the Social Democratic Party, we can only observe that its history is as yet too short to form a judgement.

Minor parties

There is not enough general experience here either upon which to base comments concerning the role of minor parties, but their potential importance, and that of independent councillors, is obvious in situations where there is no clear overall control.

If, then, our hypothetical social worker is seeking to encourage the establishment of a local welfare rights resource, she may well find one of the local political parties a fruitful channel for her efforts, especially if she is, or becomes, a member of it, and especially if it is the majority party on the council. The objective will be to build a basis of support within the local party for the idea of a welfare rights service. It is likely that party activists will be more interested in features such as advice services to the public and the capacity to mount take-up campaigns, than they will be in the more 'back-stage' activities such as advice, training and information for social services staff, but this should not present problems if the idea is to set up a service with the capacity simultaneously to perform several functions. There are good arguments for a welfare rights service which is multi-faceted: for example, where training packages are informed by casework experience.

As well as building support through the local party, contacts with individual councillors are also important, especially if the latter occupy a significant position within the policy-making machinery. This is best approached on the basis of: 'Here is a good idea : what do you think?' rather than any amateur attempt at Machiavellian string-pulling. This sort of contact will frequently be informal, perhaps in the pub after a meeting : but if such occasions do not arise, there is no reason why a specific request for a meeting to discuss the issue should not prove productive – perhaps via the local CPAG or BASW branch (whose potential roles are discussed below).

Whether it will prove helpful or counter-productive to gain the active support of minority parties, or indeed minority factions within the controlling party, will vary from place to place depending on local political relationships. In my experience, it is helpful to to have a broad base of support, but this will not always be the case in all areas or all situations: this can be a matter for fine political judgement.

All of this will be readily recognised by the reader who is familiar with the workings of the local democratic process/the wheeler-dealing of local government (whichever way you like to look at it). However, I have set it out because often social services employees (perhaps because of the professional emphasis on individual casework) are not as familiar as they might be with the way local government policy-making machinery, formal and informal, actually works.

Professional bodies, voluntary organisations and pressure groups

The role of these bodies in a situation where efforts are being made to persuade a local authority to set up a new service or resource, is perhaps fairly obvious. The various techniques of lobbying, campaigning, use of the local mass media and forming of alliances will be appropriate and necessary to varying degrees, depending on the initial receptivity of the LA. Howard (1978, p.25) stresses the part which voluntary organisations can play:

> For a policy of any description to take off, initially the conception must be planted in fertile soil. Thus, if a local authority is the most appropriate base for a welfare rights programme, from where does the initial germ of the idea spring? Local government officials cannot be discounted but, in small authorities especially, they may be so tied up with the day-to-day running of their departments, that there is little time for innovation. It is at this creative juncture that voluntary bodies may play a crucial role.

Howard perhaps underestimates the potential role of the LA bureaucracy (for both good and ill), a question which I shall consider below. She is right, though, to emphasise the potential contribution of voluntary organisations. These may be of the 'service delivery' variety (Family Service Units for example) which would be in a good position to attest to gaps in provision; or they may be of the more overtly campaigning type, such as CPAG; or perhaps community-based, such as a tenants' association. A professional body such as BASW would potentially occupy a similar strategic position. CPAG, certainly, in liaison with Labour councillors, has on a number of occasions played a role in helping to create welfare rights services. Illustrations from Newcastle, Nottinghamshire, Harlow and Manchester are given below.

Local authority management

It should be borne in mind that, if our crusading social worker is an employee of the LA which she is seeking to influence, then she may be able to take advantage of internal inputs into policy-making, either as a supplement or alternative to wider lobbying. She may also find that efforts to lobby the politicians, whether via a political party, or via CPAG or BASW or some similar channel, may be seen by SSD management as an attempt to bypass the legitimate departmental policy-making machinery, and may be resented. It is therefore as well actively to seek the support of departmental management within the LA. (For 'shorthand' purposes, I shall pursue this in the context of the SSD; but all of the points made below could also be applied to the management of other service departments.) If our social worker is open and forthright in her enthusiasm for her objective, then management, if it is worth its salary, should regard the whole thing as a constructive policy debate and not try to invoke bureaucratic orthodoxy to stifle discussion.

It should not be assumed, though, that SSD management will prove hostile or indifferent. I have referred in Chapter 3 to Holman's reports (1973, p.362) of managerial discouragement of welfare rights in the early 1970s. I expressed the hope that this problem would not be so readily encountered today. I do not, of course, expect undiluted enthusiasm, even in the big cities : for example, a news report on Birmingham, in *Community Care* (23 February 1984, p.5), remarked that the (then) director 'takes a casework view of social work and does not believe that things like community work, general advice giving, welfare rights, is any part of social work'. We can contrast this, though, with the view of Bob Winter, Strathclyde's divisional social work director for Glasgow, quoted in *Social Work Today* (1 October 1984, p.9) as observing, at a BASW study course on social work skills for the 1980s, that clients' failure to receive state benefits 'through the studied incompetence of social workers has done massive damage to their image in deprived communities'. Social workers' response to the unemployment issue 'is vital to our profession; is essential to our credibility with our communities. We really are on the line with this one'. Thus, social services management, far from being an obstacle to be overcome in developing welfare rights resources, may be vociferously in support. The possibility that local SSD management may be a potential ally, or even initiator of such efforts, should therefore be taken into account.

Even where management is initially unconvinced, it is possible to produce persuasive arguments which may bring about a change of view. The potential benefits of a welfare rights resource both directly to clients and indirectly via support of social services staff, can be stressed, as can Winter's point concerning public credibility. Moreover, welfare rights can be promoted on 'cost-effectiveness' grounds, for example in terms of the cost of keeping children in care; of making 'Section 1' payments; or (to return to housing-related matters) of rent arrears.

Other aspects of the local authority bureaucracy

It is, then, possible to discover supportive attitudes amongst, and to gain valuable backing from, senior management within the service departments. The same may also be true of policy development units and the like, centrally-based within chief executives' or analogous departments. Less promising, though, are the prospects as regards certain other sections of the LA bureaucracy, especially where proposals are advanced which would entail the employment of staff. Particularly, I have in mind the LA's personnel machinery. This may be organised centrally, in individual departments, or both, but, particularly where it is concentrated outside of the service departments themselves, may develop objectives and approaches which are at odds with those of the latter.

This question of the role of personnel bureaucracies in relation to LA policy-making and implementation is in my view an interesting and much-neglected area, which takes on particular significance at a time of severe expenditure constraints. The formal idea is that such machinery should handle questions relating to staff resources, conditions of service and so on in such a way as will best provide value for money, taking into account both cost and the effective delivery of a given level of services, bearing in mind also the need to promote good industrial relations. In practice, the remoteness of such machinery from the delivery of services can lead to the situation where the latter becomes perceived as very much a secondary consideration as against the objective of cost savings. This in turn can lead to friction with trade unions and the development of an anti-trade union perspective within the personnel machinery. In extreme cases, the combination of hostility to trade unions and opposition to increased (or commitment to reduced) public expenditure can lead to a prevalent ideology within this section of the bureaucracy which is quite at variance with that of the majority party on the council. This is how some Labour councils with a reputation for progressive approaches to service delivery can from time to time exhibit displays of hawkish labour relations practice which one would more readily expect to find amongst Councils of a very different political persuasion.

This is not to say that conflict between councillors and the personnel machinery should then be expected. Given the close association between the Labour Party and the trade union movement, many Labour councillors are uneasy with their role as employer. There is therefore a strong incentive to 'leave it to the professionals', thereby bestowing upon the personnel bureaucracy a large degree of autonomy. In terms of the establishment of new services and projects, this arrangement can be a considerable force to be reckoned with : it can lead to under-staffing, disputed gradings, pressure for temporary rather than permanent appointments, difficulty in renewing temporary contracts; all of which can make it difficult to set up a service and/or keep it running on an even keel.

Trade unions

The fact that welfare rights workers concern themselves both with the entitlements of workers involved in trade disputes, and with those of low-paid workers, tends to promote a ready co-operation between welfare rights agencies and trade unions. The extent to which trade unions, perhaps via the local Trades Council, tend to see their role as including the influencing of LA provision is another factor which will vary from area to area, but it is a possibility which could often usefully be explored in promoting the establishment of a local authority welfare rights resource.

Such considerations apply to trade unions *in general.* Those specifically having membership within the LA, such as the National and Local Government Officers' Association (NALGO) and the National Union of Public Employees (NUPE), will be relevant also from the point of view of the defence of resources which may be imperilled, for example by expenditure cuts.

Case examples: getting established and staying alive

I would like to conclude this chapter by returning to my records from Newcastle upon Tyne's Welfare Rights Service, to Howard Sharron's interviews for *Social Work Today's* 1982 'Social Security Special Feature', and to Harlow and Manchester, to illustrate the operation of some of these diverse factors in different local authorities.

Newcastle

The following examples from Newcastle serve to illustrate both the development of services, and their protection in troubled times. The Welfare Rights Service was inaugurated with one WRO in 1974, a team being established in 1976. The setting up of the Service was very much a direct result of the personal enthusiasm and interest of the (then) Chairman of the Social Services Committee (subsequently Leader of the Council) Jeremy Beecham. The initiative was also strongly supported by the local CPAG branch, one of the most active members of which – John Veit Wilson – had contributed to the formulation of 'anti-poverty' aspects of the local Labour

Party's programme prior to its regaining of control of the Council in 1974. The Service experienced slow but fairly steady growth during the 1970s and 1980s, to reach its present pattern of provision, which includes several advice centres, debt counselling projects, an 'ethnic minorities' project, information, publicity and training programmes and its own policy and management unit. Not only is there considerable support from SSD management, but the Housing Department's growing interest is reflected in its part-funding of the debt counselling initiative, which itself originated in a survey of unemployment in the East End of the City, conducted by the LA's Policy Services Department (City of Newcastle upon Tyne, 1982). The role of politicians, a pressure group and inter-departmental collaboration in the establishment and development of the Service illustrates the varied nature of the factors at work.

All has not been roses, however, and particularly instructive in relation to the *defence* of services were the events of 1979, when the Service was almost extinguished as a side-effect of the social workers' strike. The latter (concerning a pay dispute) took place in a number of LAs between 1978 and 1979 and lasted for seven months in Newcastle. An unusual feature of the strike locally was that many of the non-social work specialist staff (including WROs) were also called out. There is not space here to describe in any detail the complex events which ensued : suffice it to say that when a national settlement was finally reached, a policy of exclusion from the agreement of all non-social work specialist staff was adopted by the local personnel machinery. (This approach was endorsed by the relevant committee, but the strategic initiative – according to various sources – lay with the personnel bureaucracy.) A new welfare rights pay structure was to be imposed by means of a non-negotiable 'determination' – a structure which a subsequent national pay survey of welfare rights staff showed would be 'around £2000 a year below the average, and paying little over half as much as in the upper areas of the range' (Fimister, 1979b, p.9). A comparable position was shared by only two other LAs in the country, so the service woul clearly be faced with the staff recruitment and turnover problems confronting any organisation with pay levels radically out of line with the norm. The effect of a permanently inexperienced staff on the type of service which could be offered was certain to be highly adverse. Eventually, by the beginning of 1980, these proposals were dropped and a new structure negotiated at acceptable rates. How was such a change of heart achieved?

First, the argument concerning recruitment and so on initially made no dent on the refusal to negotiate. So the welfare rights staff insisted that NALGO declare its intention of placing an embargo upon the filling of vacant posts, such vacancies indeed occurring, not surprisingly, within a very short time. By the end of 1979, all advice centres were closed. The next group of actors to take the stage were the service's customers: community and voluntary groups; LA staff of various sorts; trade unions; all wanted to know what had gone wrong. Questions were asked at the Trades Council and representations made to the Authority. Thirdly, councillors themselves were not prepared to see the service close, this danger having been an unintended consequence of the sporadic exchanges of fire between employer and trade union sides which had continued beyond the termination of an often acrimonious strike. The instruction was therefore given to open negotiations and seek a settlement. As a local newspaper subsequently put it, in a news item titled 'City Revives Benefits Advice Unit': 'voluntary groups, tenants' organisations and councillors have been calling for the return of the service' (*Evening Chronicle*, Newcastle upon Tyne, 14 January 1980).

Strathclyde

Strathclyde provides a notable example of the effect described earlier in this chapter, whereby welfare rights is adopted by a Labour council – perhaps, as in this case, by giving a new 'slant' to an existing service – as a method and symbol of resistance to what is regarded as a hostile Conservative central government. Established in the mid-1970s and subsequently expanded greatly (see Chapter 3) from the original conception, Strathclyde Welfare Rights Service has enjoyed considerable political backing from the majority party; and can also claim support from senior management within the Social Work Department. The celebrated 1980 take-up campaign, involving mass distribution of 'claim' postcards and a lively clash with the DHSS and the government, has been described thus by Quintin Oliver, the (then) Glasgow divisional welfare rights adviser: 'the benefits postcard campaign exemplified the approach of councillors determined to use the influence of the local authority to challenge central government policy and come to the aid of ratepayers. It was a way of mobilising the community – a form of mass action against the monetarists' (quoted in Sharron, 1982, p.8).

Sharron (1982, p.8) sees the campaign as a situation in which

> hard-bitten Scottish socialists, their faces set against England's Margaret Thatcher and the 1980 Social Security Act, sought for a way to keep some of the money in the region which the Tory government were, through benefit cuts, intent upon taking out... The campaign was political dynamite. Poor Lynda Chalker was caught trying to maintain a rhetorical commitment to take-up while as a minister of a cutting government, obstructing the Strathclyde campaign. It was an untenable position, as the press was quick to let her know. She has not done very well since... One major effect of the campaign was to turn social security into a political issue among Labour Councils up and down the country.

Nottinghamshire

Sharron's round-Britain tour also took him to Nottinghamshire, where a more finely-balanced political situation (the county council being liable to changes in political control) leads to a less controversial, although nevertheless innovative, style on the part of the Welfare Rights Service. As Newcastle, Strathclyde and Nottinghamshire are all prominent contributors to the activities of the national network of welfare rights services, I am readily able to confirm Sharron's impressions of the last two organisations. As regards Nottinghamshire, he rightly draws attention to, again, the interaction of politicians, CPAG and SSD management. In the words of John Hannam, the welfare rights team leader (quoted in Sharron, 1982, p.10) :

> There was a lot of enthusiasm for the welfare rights service, not just from Labour but also from within the department...Vivienne Bell, the Chairwoman of Social Services, is a national executive member of Child Poverty Action Group, while the Director, Edward Culham, is on the Income Maintenance Panel of the Association of Directors of Social Services. As such welfare rights has always been seen as having a legitimate role within the department, and most area offices have a social worker with a special expertise on the subject. The appreciation of the importance of welfare rights has grown with the development of mass unemployment in Nottinghamshire.

The Social Services Chairwoman's CPAG connection provides an interesting parallel with Newcastle, as herein lies yet another situation where an enthusiastic senior politician, with CPAG associations and backing, has played a major role in creating a service. It should be noted, though, that in Nottinghamshire it was rather a question of reviving a service, as an earlier welfare rights post, also in the SSD, had been earmarked by the previous regime for early retirement of the post-holder and non-filling of the consequent vacancy.

Harlow and Manchester

The CPAG connection is further illustrated by the example of *Harlow*, where the Council's decision, in the mid-1970s, to set up a welfare rights service, was stimulated by the example of a CPAG welfare rights market stall which included Labour councillors amongst its volunteer staff (Bennett, 1985). This reminds us once more of *Manchester* where the CPAG branch's pioneering work on welfare rights stalls (Bull, 1970, pp.132—3) was an early stage in the process of stimulation of local political interest which led to the establishment of Manchester Welfare Rights Service.

I trust that the various illustrations above will have served to demonstrate that the political factors involved in establishing, and indeed preserving, a welfare rights resource are – as is the case with any policy innovation – likely to be diverse and subtle. If local welfare rights enthusiasts are to involve themselves in creating, improving or defending such services, then these are the elements with which they must deal, learning to recognise opportunities and pitfalls alike, to distinguish the ladders from the snakes.

5

Information Systems

If social services staff are to be effective in the welfare rights
aspects of their work, then they will need to be appropriately
trained and to be supported by good information systems.
Training is the subject of Chapter 6; here, we look at the
issues surrounding information resources.

The case for good, accessible information systems – and
for using them – is put unequivocally by Paul Burgess (1983):

> If there is one fact upon which welfare rights workers all
> agree...it is that there is no substitute for reliable sources of
> information. The point may seem self-evident. So why is it that
> so many social workers appear to operate without a single
> welfare rights guide available to them?...The infuriating thing
> is that so many people who should know better use the
> complexity of the system as an excuse for not doing anything to
> equip themselves with even the *means* to find some of the
> answers.

It is essential to recognise, though, that *management* has a
key role in ensuring that the provision of information
resources is taken seriously. Quite apart from any more lofty
considerations, there is the simple question of cost-
effectiveness, even if construed only within the context of the
telephone bill. Both Burgess and I have had occasion to make
this particular point in the pages of the social services press.
On the eve of the 1980 changes to the supplementary benefit
scheme, commenting on the challenge to social workers
which the new system presented, I argued in *Social Work
Today* (Fimister, 1980a, pp.6 – 7) that:

> Those readers who are fortunate enough to work in an area with
> some sort of accessible welfare rights advice service will be able
> to phone in for specialised advice – albeit punctuated by long
> pauses and the rustle of regulations – but there may be a
> tendency for the telephones of such agencies to be even more
> frequently engaged than usual once the effects [of the

changes] start to be felt. Written information on hand in the office would seem to be essential... Even the more financially cautious SSDs or voluntary organisations might be persuaded that here is a means of saving on expensive telephone calls and staff time.

More than two years into the new scheme, Burgess was led to conclude (as indeed one still does today) that the need to dispel managerial caution and plain lack of imagination was more pressing than ever. As the new housing benefit and statutory sick pay schemes descended upon hapless claimants and harassed advisers, Burgess (1983) wrote, in *Community Care*, of the

> managerial deficiencies regarding the information needs of social workers. It is my impression that a low priority is given in many social services departments to the information resources which social work staff need if they are to operate efficiently. This is, fundamentally, managerial short-sightedness.

He went on to cite the very low annual cost of his recommended 'shopping list' of essential handbooks (less than £12.00 p.a. at the time) and continued: 'A moment taken to compare this outlay with the *daily* cost of the telephone calls made to find out the answers which have been promised to clients illustrates the ludicrous economics employed. It is the sort of thing which gives local government a bad name.'

The experience of welfare rights advisers such as Burgess and myself is supported by research findings. Melotte (1977) reports that:

> From the responses of those interviewed it was clear that social workers lacked a single consistent source of reliable information on welfare benefits...The lack of a consistent source of up-to-date information...is clearly a situation that any social services department should take responsibility for and attempt to remedy rapidly.

Melotte recommends: 'The immediate introduction of a single system for the collation and dissemination of information about welfare benefits to "front-line" staff within the social services department'.

Becker, MacPherson and Silburn (1983, pp. 18—21) found that:

> Some at least of the basic information is circulated around the area offices although the method, extent and efficiency of this circulation seems to be fairly haphazard and to vary considerably from one office to another...45 per cent of those who answered said that the information they might need was hard to come by, and a further 7 per cent that the supply was totally inadequate. There would seem to be scope for administrative measures to improve the supply and effective use of sources...A number of respondents complained that much of the material that might be found in the office was out of date.

While standards of information provision clearly leave a good deal to be desired in many areas, managers in more forward-looking SSDs and other social services agencies have recognised the importance of reliable and up-to-date information and have allocated resources accordingly. Nevertheless, we are not simply in a position of seeking to extend such good practice: current and increasingly severe financial constraints will put departmental budgets for such items under growing pressure, and it will be necessary to defend them, stressing, amongst others, arguments along the lines of those advanced above.

Before going on to look in more detail at printed information, something should be said concerning the availability of advice by telephone. For our present purposes, we are of course concerned with advice available to social services staff rather than to the general public although in practice the two may be part of the same facility.

Advice by telephone

However comprehensive a printed information system may be, it cannot cater for every circumstance, especially when a case is complex, perhaps involving a number of interacting variables, or when a negotiating or appeal *strategy* needs to be discussed in subtle detail. A local welfare rights unit which is able to provide advice by telephone will therefore play a valuable role in the scheme of things. Some social services staff may indeed be located in close proximity to such a unit, which could provide the opportunity to call round in person and discuss tricky cases in some detail. For most, though, a telephone link will be necessary.

Ideally, social services staff would seek to find the necessary answers in the office information system, and resort to telephone advice as and when the former proved insufficient to the task. I have discussed in Chapter 3 the danger that some staff may become over-dependent on a welfare rights resource, and use of the telephone line can be a main aspect of this: so the idea that the 'advice line' is to be seen as a *supplement* to the office-based information system should be actively promoted. It should be added that, from the client's point of view, the adviser who is over-dependent on direct help by welfare rights staff is far more useful than he or she who is unaware of the need for, or who for some other reason does not seek the necessary welfare rights information. Nor should, for example, a knowledgeable social worker feel that it is in any way an admission of failure to need to seek further advice: social security is a complex business; and full time welfare rights specialists themselves have their work cut out to keep up-to-date, will readily acknowledge their own dependence on their information systems and do not hesitate themselves to consult colleagues.

A welfare rights advice line should be available throughout the working day at least (and of course there are fairly obvious arguments which can be advanced in favour of 'out-of-hours' services). Many of the existing services are able to operate their telephone advice lines part-time only and this to some extent defeats the object: social services staff will frequently be seeking advice on an urgent basis perhaps with the client waiting in the office, so a tape-recorded message giving details of the next session will not be a lot of use. Small scale and/or highly pressured welfare rights units may be able to allocate such modest staff resources to the telephone line that sickness, holidays and other unavoidable commitments may lead to considerable unreliability. Those providing, and those subscribing to welfare rights advisory services, will need to ponder such considerations carefully.

I should briefly refer to 'live' information media other than the telephone. There is no doubt that recent and rapid advances in communications technology offer the potential to revolutionise information provision to public and advisers alike. Exploratory work is already under way in the welfare rights field. This is a very large subject in itself and one which may seem a little remote to social services staff who, in the present financial climate, may need to deploy a medium-sized campaign just to obtain a replacement note pad. I therefore do not propose to pursue this question in any detail here. Suffice it to say that the day should not be far off when the dog-eared handbook, overlaid with numerous handwritten amendments, will be to a great extent replaced by the shiny and up-to-the-minute visual display unit.

I turn now to the office information package.

The office-based information system

During the 1970s and 1980s, the available range of welfare rights or more general benefit information steadily expanded, so that a considerable scope for choice has now replaced the famine of good material which prevailed in earlier years. In attempting to identify the sort of information system which will be appropriate to the social services setting, it is necessary to try to establish some guiding principles. The following are key considerations.

How ambitious?

I promised in Chapter 1 that I would 'avoid suggesting systems which are expensive or difficult to maintain and shall not be suggesting that you should kit out your area team sub-office as if it were a law centre'. I shall endeavour here to keep that promise. Thus, I shall regard the main volumes of social security legislation (with the possible exception of that relating to supplementary benefit), social security encyclo-paedias and the like, as being more relevant to the advice centre than to the less specialised social services context. Readers interested in developing a more ambitious system than that which I describe below should consult an established and well-resourced advice centre to discuss the matter.

How extensive?

I would argue that the system should be based on a relatively small number of regularly-updated handbooks. Experience suggests that these are more easily made use of, in most practical settings, than are other forms of printed information. They can be comprehensive while being easily transported around an office; and the information is contained in a compact form without the necessity to shuffle through, for example, several file boxes full of bulletins or journals. I have frequently asked social workers and other 'non-specialist' advisers about their practical requirements in this respect, and there is no doubt that the 'handbook' approach is the most popular, if their responses are anything to go by.

If follows that other forms of information should be seen as supplementary to the main system: there are a number of journals (for example, the *Journal of Social Welfare Law, Legal Action, Roof* and various others) which can usefully enhance the main information resources. The main social work journals also have welfare rights columns ('Benefits' in *Social Work Today*; 'In Benefit' in *Community Care*) which can be extracted and kept on file. There is also a role for locally-produced bulletins and leaflets. It is essential, though, that such material should be well organised and maintained; that users should be aware of the dangers of obsolescence; and that users are also clear on which are intended to be the main items and which are supplementary: a massive pile of 'bumph' can discourage people from going near any of it.

In approaching my task in writing this chapter, I have decided against reviewing or setting out the above additional material in any detail. This is because the approach of this book very much revolves around the idea of influencing policy-makers to implement or at least explore, certain practical measures; or of persuading practitioners, educators and others to press for them. I would therefore like to place great emphasis on my list of 'essentials' and do not wish to obscure it by writing a lengthy (and possibly boring) account of the large amount of supplementary material which is available. I leave it to the reader to pursue such researches *after* he or she is satisfied that the problem of the basic essentials has been solved locally.

How up-to-date?

In recent years, the social security system has been in a more or less continuous state of change. Annually-updated material is required at the very least and in practice, every effort has to be made to identify significant changes and annotate the handbooks accordingly. Here, supplementary bulletins can be very useful, provided that somebody has the time and know-how to undertake the annotation (see 'organisation' below). I therefore do not include in my list of essentials certain useful and well-written sources which are *not* annually updated: examples would be Ogus and Barendt's *The Law of Social Security*; or Lynes' *Penguin Guide to Supplementary Benefits*. These are in fact well worth having and I would recommend them to readers: but the 'dating' problem renders them more suitable for the 'supplementary' category, except for the period following the appearance of new editions (and, in the case of Ogus and Barendt, supplements). This limitation applies to a number of useful textbooks currently on the market.

How detailed?

For our purposes here, it is essential that handbooks should be sufficiently detailed and precise and should make adequate use of specific legal references. The latter consideration inevitably detracts from 'readability', but is essential if the guide is to serve its purpose for the front-line adviser or advocate. Knowing that a claimant is entitled to a particular payment under the terms of the relevant regulations may be of little value if the adviser does not know exactly which regulations and a DHSS adjudication officer takes a contrary view. One can hardly argue that 'it must be right because my rights guide says so': the adjudication officer will not be impressed.

Thus, several useful handbooks currently on the market are best seen as guides for use by more general advisers or claimants who will be seeking more specialist help before taking matters further. I have not usually included these in my list of essentials (except in some instances where the guide has other strong merits) as I am by definition concerned with the adviser who will be dealing directly with the benefit-administering agencies.

I would like now to set out my list of 'essential items' for the office-based information system and deal briefly with DHSS leaflets, before turning to the crucial question of the organisation of such a system.

The main items

Some readers will undoubtedly consider that I have inexcusably omitted certain items. Views as to what is or is not indispensable to particular types of adviser can provoke lively differences of opinion. However, I am confident that the majority of the sources set out below would be pinpointed by virtually any welfare rights specialist, whatever other variations he or she might propose.

Details of prices are obviously transient, so I shall not give them, except to say that all but the first two are relatively cheap: for example, the CPAG handbooks are £4.00 each at the time of writing. The first two items are not handbooks and are somewhat more expensive, the price varying depending on the number of supplements currently required. I shall give current details of the agencies publishing the various items and enquiries can then be made of them to obtain up-to-date information. It should be noted that some of these agencies offer subscriptions of various sorts, whereby the handbooks can be obtained along with other useful material. For example, CPAG has several different subscriptions, various policy, research and welfare rights material, including the *Welfare Rights Bulletin,* being available as well as the handbooks. Similarly, a subscription to the Disability Alliance can take in the *Disability Rights Bulletin*. Both of these bulletins, it should be noted, play a valuable role in permitting their corresponding handbooks to be updated between editions. Details will change, so enquiries should be made of the publishing organisation in each case. If direct subscriptions are not obtained, then the time to look out for new editions is round about the main benefit uprating date.

The Law Relating to Supplementary Benefits and Family Income Supplements

Supplementary benefit is such an important and frequently-encountered area for social services agencies, and is now so heavily dependent on regulations, that there is a strong case for having the source material even within non-specialist settings. Known, after the colour of its glowing cover, as the 'Yellow Book' (possibly a symbol of the retreat from the objectives of 1948?) this volume contains the raw material of skirmishes with adjudication officers. I would add an important qualification, though, to my recommendation: this is a loose-leaf volume which is periodically updated by supplements (which are automatically sent and separately invoiced following initial purchase of the main volume). It uses an elaborate page numbering system to facilitate the insertion of supplements, and updating the system is therefore a moderately skilled administrative/clerical task. Errors are cumulative as subsequent supplements fail to 'fit' and a very badly cared for volume may have to be thrown away and the system started again from the beginning. Agencies severely lacking in administrative/clerical resources may therefore be best advised to confine their investment to the handbooks. Or an alternative approach to this legislation may be to invest in John Mesher's annotated version, *CPAG's Supplementary Benefit and Family Income Supplement: the Legislation*. This volume reproduces the relevant law and has the great advantage of explanatory comment and cross-references, for example, to Social Security Commissioners' decisions. As it is to be revised annually, Mesher's volume does provide a viable alternative to a 'Yellow Book' subscription. Details of Mesher can be obtained from Sweet and Maxwell, Spon. (Booksellers) Ltd, North Way, Andover, Hants, SP1O 5BE. Details of the 'Yellow Book' can be obtained from Her Majesty's Stationery Office (HMSO), various branches.

The 'S' Manual

This is another loose-leaf system, this time consisting of voluminous instructions used by DHSS officers to operate the supplementary benefit scheme. The advantages of having these to hand are obvious. Note, though, that the same comments concerning the updating system apply as in the case of the 'Yellow Book'. Details this time are from the DHSS Leaflets Unit, PO Box 21, Stanmore, Middlesex, HA7 1AY.

National Welfare Benefits Handbook

This is published by CPAG, 1 Macklin Street, Drury Lane, London, WC2B 5NH, and really is an essential item. It concentrates on means-tested benefits, with particularly detailed sections on supplementary and housing benefits. There are the exact references to the legislation necessary if battle is to be joined effectively with the benefit-administering bodies and into its fifteenth edition at the time of writing, this is a guide which embodies the advantages of considerable experience.

Rights Guide to Non-Means-Tested Social Security Benefits

Published by CPAG, this is the companion volume to the above, covering the contributory 'National Insurance' benefits, and non-means-tested, non-contribution-tested benefits such as child benefit and the non-contributory benefits for disabled people. It has the same virtues as its counterpart and should likewise be regarded as indispensable.

Supplementary Benefits Handbook

This is published by the DHSS, and details are obtainable from HMSO. Misleadingly sub-titled 'a guide to claimants' rights', it is in fact nothing of the sort, being rather an explanation of the DHSS interpretation of the supplementary benefit legislation. As such, it is highly useful, especially to those lacking the '*S*' *Manual,* and indeed is more portable and perhaps easier to use than the latter, although nothing like as detailed.

A Guide to Housing Benefits

Published jointly by the Institute of Housing, 12 Upper Belgrave Street, London, SW1X 8BA; and SHAC (The London Housing Aid Centre), 189a Old Brompton Road, London, SW5 0AR, this is a detailed guide to one of the most notoriously complicated areas of the benefit system. Born of the chaos surrounding the introduction of the housing benefit scheme in 1982 – 3, this publication clearly has a busy future.

Disability Rights Handbook

Published by the Disability Alliance Educational and Research Association, 25 Denmark Street, London, WC2H 8NJ, this is a comprehensive guide to benefits and services for disabled people. Like the other remaining items on this list, it derives its particular usefulness from the close focus which is permitted by concentration on a particular client group.

Your Rights for Pensioners

Published by Age Concern, Bernard Sunley House, 60 Pitcairn Road, Mitcham, Surrey, CR4 3LL. A guide focusing particularly on the welfare rights of elderly people.

Housing and Supplementary Benefits: a Rights Guide for Single Homeless People, Boarders and Hostel Residents

Published by CHAR (the Campaign for Single Homeless People), 5 – 15 Cromer Street, London, WC1H 8LS. Another specialised guide which, given that members of the client group in question tend to be particularly subject to the neglect and disregard of their rights, benefits especially from its attention to legal chapter and verse.

DHSS leaflets

Finally, although I indicated above that I regarded handbooks, rather than leaflets, as the most useful focus of the information system, I should say something about the role of DHSS leaflets. These are useful to have around to give to claimants who have specific queries about particular benefits, especially where they may need an application form attached to the leaflet. But I must confess that I am not enthusiastic about these as part of the type of information system in question here. They are difficult to distribute and keep in order, partly as a result of their large number and partly because of their highly obscure numbering system, which is likely to confuse the most assiduous, especially given that correction or amendment slips are sent out with no leaflet or subject title. They have, moreover, traditionally suffered from 'tunnel vision', dealing with individual benefits in isolation. The DHSS has sought to tackle the latter problem with its more recent 'FB' ('family benefit') series, but these are very general and of little value for specialist reference purposes. Nevertheless, DHSS leaflets seem to be looked to as a more or less automatic requirement of an information system and so, provided that care is taken with updating, replacement and filing, I shall cautiously endorse them as a supplementary item to the main system. It should, of course, be borne in mind that they are 'official' in perspective, setting out details of what should, and not necessarily what does, happen in the real world and certainly not providing strategies for advocacy, but within these limitations the information can undoubtedly be helpful. DHSS leaflets are free of charge, although the application system is characteristically confusing: individual copies of each new leaflet or new edition can be obtained as they are issued, by arrangement with the Information Division, DHSS, Alexander Fleming House, Elephant and Castle, London, SE1 6BY; while orders for bulk supplies on a 'one-off' basis, for example for distribution to clients, should be placed with the DHSS Leaflets Unit, address as for the *'S' Manual* subscription above.

Different agencies may have different requirements as regards the subject focus of their information systems. But if the system is constructed from some combination of the above, regarding the two CPAG handbooks as especially indispensable, then a solid foundation will have been laid.

Information systems, though, will not look after themselves. I shall turn now to the vital area of overall system organisation.

Organisation

I shall describe the issues here in terms of a fairly large agency – say, a SSD with a number of area offices, day centres, hospital social work units and so on. Smaller organisations will frequently have fewer problems in the effective dissemination of information, but unless the agency is very small, the principles will be generally similar. I shall also assume that a welfare rights unit exists within the SSD, acting as a resource for other social services staff. We have seen that, in practice, such a unit may be within another department or indeed outside the LA altogether, but again, the broad principles apply. More difficult is the unfortunate but widespread situation where no welfare rights resource exists. Here, some other individual or unit within the organisation will have to handle the servicing and co-ordinating roles described: perhaps a research unit or training section. This will inevitably raise problems in the absence of a specialist knowledge of the material, but it may be the best option available in areas which are lacking in welfare rights provision.

An effective approach to setting-up an office information system must entail constantly bearing in mind the practical requirements of the working situation. Material which is inaccessible will be under-used or not used at all. A good example is the question of location of the system and the need to have an information package on each *site*. It is not good enough, for example, simply to provide a package for each section of the SSD, according to some bureaucratic definition of organisational structure. In practice, on the ground, the information system must be within easy reach of the people who will be using it. This point is obvious when an area team, say, is split into more than one office: but less immediately apparent is the position in, for example, a hospital, which may consist of one building, but where long corridors may intervene between the working settings of different groups of social services staff. These groups may be quite small, or there may be indeed one social worker attached to a specialist unit, but these must be considered separate sites and information packages provided accordingly, if the agency is serious in its intention to provide for the welfare rights aspects of the job. There is of course a case for holding some larger and expensive items, such as the 'Yellow Book', on fewer sites, but generally this principle should be applied.

It would be possible for each sub-division of the organisation (in our example, of the SSD) to handle its own ordering of the elements of the information system, direct from the publishers. This would indeed have certain advantages in terms of shortening the chain of communication. However, it would also entail considerable multiplication of paperwork and is unlikely to be seen by departmental management as a cost-effective approach. Some units could also be too small to handle the administration; while this approach would also forego the wider communication possibilities which a linked distribution network can create (see below).

Thus, the most promising approach is to handle ordering

and distribution of material centrally, new and updated material being gathered and sent out to the different sites by – in our example – the SSD's welfare rights unit. The latter should approach this task dynamically, supplementing the elements of the main system with lively covering letters, 'one-off' leaflets, newsletters, details of training opportunities: in other words, seeking to sustain a 'live' system of communications, rather than merely a boring administrative process. This system can be combined with some individual direct subscriptions and ordering by the individual sites themselves, where they have specialised requirements or particular priorities not shared by the members of the wider network.

On each site, there should be an 'information contact' who will receive the information package, organise, file and generally look after it, identifying any missing items and seeking replacements from the welfare rights unit, ensuring that updating material, annotations etc are correctly inserted, and so on. This task should again be approached dynamically, active attention being paid to how well the package is working in the office: do people know where it is, how to use it? Is it comprehensive enough for their needs? There must be feedback to the welfare rights unit, not just to seek replacements but to give specific 'consumer feedback', offering ideas and suggestions.

The role of 'information contact' should not be shared, but should be undertaken by one, named person: otherwise the process will become neglected, fragmented or both. The information contact could be a social worker, home help organiser, manager, administrative officer, but the individual must be an enthusiast: conscripts should be avoided if the necessary enthusiasm is to be generated. To handle the information contact role as a routine clerical function is a mistake. It should be noted, though, that the contact must also have the ability to look after the system: not everybody finds that a systematic approach to the handling of information comes naturally to him or her, and certainly expensive mistakes can be made if items such as the 'Yellow Book' and *'S' Manual* are included.

I should add that, in the case of some of the more

important handbooks, the office need not be seen as the smallest target of distribution. Fieldwork staff can usefully maintain a small information package in a car, and there is a very strong case in particular for issuing all relevant staff with individual copies of the *National Welfare Benefits Handbook.*

It is at the level of 'information contact' that the above type of system is most likely to go wrong. I shall therefore devote some space below to outlining the most common varieties of pitfall. Before doing so, though, I would like briefly to describe some of the considerable wider possibilities which derive from this sort of distribution network. A communications system that links together welfare rights enthusiasts within a wide range of social services settings, ideally drawing in all relevant sections within the organisation, must have greater potential than simply the distribution of information. It may be possible, then, for the welfare rights unit to convene periodic meetings of the information contacts. Initially and perhaps primarily these can be used to discuss the content and operation of the information system. But other possibilities can be developed, such as the discussion of training requirements and perhaps the setting up of joint research initiatives or joint campaigns aimed at improving benefit-administering policy or practice (see Chapter 7). For example, in Newcastle the network of information contacts has developed into a 'Welfare Rights/Social Work Liaison Group'. This meets quarterly and is currently looking at a proposed series of leaflets (to be produced by the Welfare Rights Service and aimed at social workers and other staff) on supplementary benefit single payments and additional requirements. It is also considering social workers' training needs; and possible measures to persuade certain local DHSS offices to set up 'working practices' liaison groups. It is attended by the more enthusiastic from amongst the information contacts and cannot claim universal participation, but it is generally regarded as having a potentially productive future.

And now, the bad news.

How not to run a system

I have suggested above that the level of the system at which things are most likely to go wrong is that of the information contact at the area office or analogous location. This is not surprising given these offices' potentially quite large numbers and considerable diversity: it can be difficult for a central information-distributing unit to recognise quickly that something has gone wrong at one of several outlying sites. For example, a social worker calling a telephone advice line with a query which could easily have been looked up in a handbook, may be thought to be shirking the effort of using an index, when the reality may be that the office information system has deteriorated or even disappeared. The types of malpratice which can give rise to such a situation can be listed under four main headings. I shall set these out below and illustrate them with 'real life' examples, although I shall not identify the SSD involved in each case, so as to spare the blushes of those concerned.

The hierarchically correct approach

Here, the manager of an office insists that the information package is addressed to him or her personally, rather than to a named individual amongst the staff. It is then dealt with in 'the normal way'. In one office where the manager insisted on this approach, social workers telephoning the welfare rights unit maintained that they had no idea where to find the information system. The hierarchically correct approach is a manifestation of a wider bureaucratic convention whereby correspondence is conducted in the name of the head of the organisation. Managers often think that this makes the department look 'official' and business-like, not realising that the public may find it impersonal and irritating. In the specific context of information systems, this approach is linked to (being one cause of) the second malpractice on my list.

The routine filing task

Here, the maintenance of the information system is seen as just another clerical task, consisting of documents to be filed. Positive efforts to arouse interest and make sure the system 'works' within the office are unlikely to fit into this approach, as is still less the provision of 'feedback' to the welfare rights unit. In one office where this approach prevailed, it eventually transpired that social workers not only did not know where the information system was, but they did not know that they had one. Nor, once apprised by the welfare rights unit of its existence, could they find it, even after a search. They had to be given a new one.

Conscript labour

This approach involves the appointment of a non-enthusiast to the information contact role. It has all the drawbacks of the 'routine filing task' approach without the advantages of any clerical expertise. Several examples of poorly-maintained and difficult-to-find systems could be cited as illustrations of the consequences. In one office, the 'conscript' was so unsure what to do with the system that it ended up in a leaflet rack in the waiting room, whence it rapidly disappeared. To look on the bright side, at least in this case one trusts that some claimants will have derived some benefit from the material: we should perhaps see it as unconscious foray into community self-help on the part of the office concerned.

The 'personal property' approach

Here, the information contact comes to be regarded as the 'owner' of the system, rather than as the person who maintains it and makes it available to the office in general. This can have several possible effects. It may simply mean that one person in the office has virtually exclusive use of the system. Sometimes, when the contact moves elsewhere, such is his or her identification with the information system that it does not occur to the office to nominate a successor and inform the welfare rights unit (which can, indeed, happen under any approach as a consequence of managerial forgetfulness). There is then nobody to maintain the system and it is likely to accumulate in a cupboard somewhere. There have even been instances where, the contact having left, administrative staff have proceeded regularly to forward material to him or her at the new address. In one area, the social services area team was split into several 'patches', and it was not uncommon for staff to relocate between them. Due to this 'mail forwarding' effect, a situation was eventually uncovered where one office enjoyed several packages and others had none.

The above malfunctions will, I am sure, be recognised by any readers who are themselves involved in information distribution via this sort of system. They result in information packages which may be hard to find or missing altogether; which may be out-of-date, incomplete or otherwise badly-maintained; and which contrast sharply with those of offices where the system is run properly. Happily, I could give many examples of the latter, including offices which will readily harass the welfare rights unit if any delay in obtaining new editions of handbooks is suspected.

One lesson of the above is very clear. It is that a considerable responsibility lies with 'on-site' management to ensure that the system is operated properly at their end.

A number of ingredients is therefore required if social services staff are to be equipped with 'the tools for the job'. First, here is a graphic illustration of the need to invest in a local welfare rights resource in order to service the overall system. Secondly, there must be a willingness to invest in the information materials themselves. Thirdly, management at all levels must be ready to give its active backing not only to the setting up of the structure, but also to its efficient operation in practice. Finally, of course, social services staff themselves must have the enthusiasm and commitment to make use of welfare rights information resources. They are more likely to feel such motivation if the system is reliably and efficiently provided.

6

Training

Information systems are an important aspect of the resources needed by social services staff if they are to function effectively in the welfare rights field. But information will not, in itself, suffice: it must be underpinned by adequate training. As welfare rights is a varied and rapidly-changing field, an approach to training must, moreover, consider the whole picture and the need to provide continuing support over time. We are, then, concerned not only with the content of professional courses, but also with continuing programmes of in-service training to take account of new material and the need for 'refresher' sessions. Infrequent, and especially 'once-only' training will not fit the bill : it has to be said that the token welfare rights input which one too often encounters on professional courses and in working settings suggests that the planners of training programmes have either not understood the problem or are not taking it seriously enough.

I am of course aware that there is currently a much wider debate under way in relation to the content and structure of training in the social services field, including an argument concerning the role and future of the Certificate of Qualification in Social Work (CQSW) and of the Certificate in Social Service (CSS). I do not propose to enter this fray : suffice it to say that *whatever* the overall structure of training in the social services, the nature of the problems with which such services must deal requires that welfare rights should constitute a significant element.

Content, objectives and methods

What should be the content, objectives and methods of welfare rights training courses? The content will of course vary with the definition of 'welfare rights'. That adopted in this book focuses on questions of income rights (see Chapter 1), which will include considerations of low pay and tax as well as the obvious areas of social security and welfare benefits. Overlap with certain services where remissions of charges are involved, and with areas such as employment law and fuel debts, are very likely. While definitions will vary, it is not hard to identify a central core. Some illustrative examples of the content of different training programmes are given later in this chapter.

Certain of the objectives of welfare rights training will be obvious : the imparting of the necessary practical knowledge and skills must be a key aim, bearing in mind the extent to which it is expected that social workers may be called upon to venture along Bull's advocacy continuum (see Chapter 2). Partly related to this, and partly to questions concerning the achievement of a wider understanding of social, political and historical context, is the argument as to the degree to which issues such as the nature of poverty and the mechanics of social deprivation should be seen as part of welfare rights training. Different commentators have different emphases.

These issues concerning training objectives surfaced in the debate on welfare rights which took place in the social work press in the early 1970s. John Cypher and Ron Walton (1973, pp.394 and 397) for example, argue that:

> An overall objective might be stated as to sensitise the student to the appropriateness of the welfare rights dimension in social work...In such a course on welfare rights time will be devoted to familiarising students with the range of benefits and services available. A knowledge of appeals procedures will also be of importance. However, the changing nature of benefits makes it of less value for the student to commit too much detail to memory. More important is that the student should know where to obtain such information when it is required and this in turn, might depend on his acceptance of welfare rights activity, however conceived, as an integral part of practice.

In the same issue of *Social Work Today*, Rosalind Brooke (1973, pp.393 – 4) discusses various different approaches to course content and teaching methods, but lays appropriate stress on the need for teachers themselves to be adequately prepared : 'A vast amount of technical detail has therefore to be accumulated and understood by the lecturer. In order to be accurate it must be kept up to date'. She goes on to argue for a wide interpretation of what constitutes welfare rights education and training:

> One of the chief functions of a welfare rights course should be to encourage and stimulate social workers to understand and question social policy and its implementation on the basis of their and their clients' experiences, and to press for social reform... Welfare rights courses should enable social workers to acquire the knowledge, skills and motivation to ensure a greater measure of justice and equality for their clients.

Holman (1973, p.363) is likewise ambitious. Welfare rights training on social work courses 'can be used not only to convey the practical details but also... as a means through which the nature of poverty, the objectives of social policy, the roles of social workers and the organisational structure of agencies can be studied'.

More recently, Becker (1983, p.52) reminds us that particular approaches require particular skills. If advocacy, rather than merely passive advice-giving is intended, then courses must take account of this :

> Whilst welfare rights work generally is increasingly being expected of social workers by clients, the role of advocacy is still alien to much of social workers' current practice... Advocacy is a particularly important element of welfare rights work, requiring its own skills (and training) and one which has been given little attention within social work or welfare rights literature.

This is a good example of the need to consider teaching methods as well as course content and objectives. Advice-giving will often be of little value without at least individual advocacy to back it up; and here role-playing techniques and videos are likely to be more appropriate tools than the straight lecture or seminar. Welfare rights teaching also benefits from the use of practical exercises – hypothetical claimants' problems to be worked out – which can even generate a certain fascination once the initial shock of having to use a calculator has been overcome : it should be borne in mind that the calculation of benefit entitlement does bear some resemblance to some of the more abstruse board games. Has Brown over there remembered to add on to eligible rent the surplus of fixed heating charge over the notional scale rate fuel element when calculating housing benefit supplement? It can be quite exciting.

I have of course merely outlined the issues : there is considerable scope for debate as to the range, shape and nature of appropriate welfare rights teaching for social services staff. One would like to think that, especially in today's social conditions, this debate is being hotly pursued and vigorously translated into practice, in training agencies up and down the country. But is it? Evidence relating to CQSW courses (there seems to be little information on other aspects of training) suggests that there is cause for concern. I would like to look at this, firstly in the context of professional training courses, before going on to consider induction and in-service training.

Is there cause for concern?

Perhaps I could open this question by taking one particular example – fairly obscure, if important in itself, but illustrative of the assumptions which are often made concerning social work training and welfare rights. One of the many and various situations in which social workers require welfare rights knowledge is that in which the parents of a child in care should be, but are not, receiving supplementary benefit or family income supplement. Quite apart from the obvious need for entitlements to be realised, and leaving aside the question of whether the child would be in care in the first place had the family not been living below the poverty line, there is the immediate need to ensure that that family is not subject to charges towards the child's upkeep while in public care. Under the terms of the Health and Social Services and Social Security Adjudications Act

1983, families on either of these benefits are exempt from charges.

I mention this in the present context having been struck by the following observation made by the Family Rights Group (Weir, 1984, p.3), in a report on charging policies for children in care circulated to Directors of Social Services and Chairpersons of Social Services Committees:

> The exemption for families on supplementary benefit and FIS will protect many poor families but it is well known that not all the families eligible actually receive these benefits. The official DHSS estimate is that take-up of FIS is only 50 per cent of eligible families. Social workers are poorly trained in welfare rights, and cannot be relied upon to identify families who should be receiving either of the two benefits.

This is a very bald statement concerning the reliability of social workers' welfare rights training : but is it justified? Unfortunately, there is evidence which strongly suggests that, generally, it is. For example, Melotte's study (1977, p.17) of one SSD found as follows:

> In order to get some idea of the level of knowledge of social workers about welfare benefits the replies to specific questions about benefits were scored and then added up to create a total for each respondent. The maximum possible total was 18. The average score for all respondents was 9.6 (53 per cent) with a range from two to 15...The possession of a CQSW qualification seemed to make no appreciable difference. The average score was 54 per cent for those with CQSW and 51 per cent for those without...Of particular concern is the 41 per cent score of those workers who had been in social services for less than a year...There are implications here for the provision of induction courses for new social workers which include information on welfare benefits.

Commenting on the apparent lack of impact of the CQSW on the problem, Melotte adds: 'There are implications here, nationally, for social work training courses to concentrate more on the theory and practice of welfare benefits work'.

The findings of Becker, MacPherson and Silburn (1983, pp.15 – 17 and 39) do not reassure:

> A substantial number of social workers, 18 per cent of our

sample, say that they have never received welfare rights training of any kind whatever. Most respondents however had some formal training, most frequently as a part of their professional training courses; two thirds of the sample referred to this. Of these, 31 people (18 per cent) had built upon this foundation by attending additional courses...A much smaller group...13.5per cent...had not had any welfare rights material in their professional training courses, but had attended some additional or in-service training course with a welfare rights content. Thus about four respondents out of five had received some welfare rights training of some kind at some time, but for nearly half of the sample this was confined to a rather minor element in their professional training courses...[in which] in very few cases did the welfare rights element exceed ten hours of instruction. For so substantial and complex a subject this is quite obviously an inadequate amount of time.

Encouragingly, the researchers found a fair degree of enthusiasm for welfare rights training amongst the social workers themselves: 'almost every worker, when asked to comment on training, said they would support increased training in welfare rights'.

Some of the most valuable recent information in this area has been provided by Steve McGrail (1983a; 1983b) of Stirling University, in his 1982 survey of welfare rights teaching on postgraduate CQSW courses in the UK. He uncovered a picture of very considerable variation and ambivalence. Time spent on welfare rights teaching varied from one to thirty-three hours, the median being ten hours. The five courses which provided more than twenty hours give us some grounds for hope; while those which offer ten hours or less must cast serious doubt on their organisers' appreciation of what is going on out there in working-class communities and of the nature of the challenge it presents to social work practice. The depth of teaching and the enthusiasm behind it also seem, from McGrail's survey, to vary considerably. What has all this done for social workers' confidence and skills in welfare rights?

McGrail refers to Parsloe and Stevenson's finding (1978) that students tended to feel adequately trained to deal with financial problems. Not surprisingly in view of his findings,

McGrail observes (1983a, p.2) that it is 'uncertain...how much significance can be attached to this judgement'. However, I would argue that there is also an historical factor to be taken into account here, as Parsloe and Stevenson's study pre-dates the radical overhaul of large areas of the social security system brought about by the 1980 and subsequent legislation, notably in the areas of supplementary and housing benefits. Social workers' confidence may not be so solid today; and certainly findings such as these suggest that it should not be. The new legislation has all but ended the role of the 'common sense case' in social security advocacy, and even the most 'ordinary' situations are now bound up in complex legislation and case law. To rely on a few hours' training on a professional course already disappearing into the mists of memory is unlikely to sustain confidence for very long in the future.

The effects of the recent major changes in the social security system have yet to make themselves fully felt. However, some further insights into students' perceptions of welfare rights teaching and practice are provided by Martin Davies's 1983 survey of 148 CQSW holders who acquired their qualification in 1980 (Davies, 1984). One part of this exercise compared students' ranking of different social work tasks in terms of their perceived importance in practice, with the success of their training in preparing them to accomplish these tasks. There was in fact a high correspondence between importance in practice and success in preparation – with one exception: 'Only the teaching of welfare rights was out of position. It was ranked as being fourth most important in practice, but came bottom of the list of the six tasks for which the students said they had been adequately prepared.' The study further records that only 43 per cent of respondents felt that they had been 'adequately prepared...to advise clients about their legal rights'; and only 36 per cent 'to fight for the client's rights'.

There are thus serious doubts as to how far the social work training system has an adequate grip on reality here. One of Davies's prescriptions (1984, p.17) is to 'raise the quality and status of course teaching of law and welfare rights'; while McGrail (1983a, p.12) concludes that there is a need for welfare rights to be given more importance in the training of social workers. In this, central controlling bodies like CCETSW might give a lead in adopting a far more vigorous and positive approach than has been taken in the past; the courses themselves perhaps need to re-evaluate the way they see welfare rights work, the resources they allocate to teaching it and the encouragement they give to their students to practise it.

One can only concur. Other evidence, from research and from experience, supports the above analyses (for example, Jacobs's findings, cited below in the context of current CCETSW initiatives). What can be done about it?

CPAG's evidence to Barclay was

> unhappy at the present state of welfare benefits teaching on CQSW courses. We know from having been involved in the provision of such teaching that welfare benefits is often seen as an appendage to 'what the course is really about'. Few social administration departments employ specialists in the field and the teaching is often sub-contracted out for a minimum number of sessions or is covered by a lecturer whose own field of interest is elsewhere...The larger teaching departments should...employ welfare benefits specialists on their staff if necessary redeploying resources within their limited budgets. The smaller ones should perhaps be encouraged to group together to employ a specialist collectively. Since welfare benefits is a highly practical area of activity, there should be some experimentation with a joint academic/social services department appointment. (Smith, 1981, p.19)

CPAG's point concerning resources and limited budgets is an important one at a time when public expenditure restrictions are striking also at educational and training resources, limiting options and consequently stifling initiative and prospects of new developments. It is interesting to note how gloom on this account pervades recent research focusing on the current plans and aspirations of social work teachers (Richards, 1984). We should be under no illusions as to the extent to which a reorganisation of priorities is made far more difficult when severe budget constraints exert their chilly grip on the whole process of course planning. Nevertheless, the question of the underdevelopment of such a key and ever more pressing teaching area as welfare rights will not go away: the nettle will have to be grasped. Are there any signs of progress?

Signs of progress?

One member of the BASW Poverty Panel told me emphatically that 'I should like to see a situation where social workers cannot emerge from social work training unless they are reasonably equipped to deal with the benefits and rights problems of the poorer-off' (Bennett, 1984a).

He was looking forward to the prospect that, at the then forthcoming 1984 BASW Annual General Meeting, something suitably solid might be agreed concerning the pressing need to make progress in this area. While one suspects that members of the Poverty Panel might have preferred something more specific, a resolution couched in general but reasonably strong terms was indeed subsequently passed unanimously by BASW's annual gathering, worded as follows:

> This Annual General Meeting stresses the importance of social workers being able to advise on welfare rights and:
>
> (a) calls upon the Central Council for Education and Training in Social Work to ensure that appropriate units of study in social security, welfare rights advocacy and debt counselling feature in submissions made by CQSW courses and CSS schemes; and
> (b) requests those organisations employing social workers to make available up-to-date information and comment on welfare rights, both to social workers and their clients. (British Association of Social Workers, 1984)

Moving this resolution, Graham Thompson observed that : 'Social workers face the reality of unemployment every day yet they do not have enough knowledge of welfare rights to give practical advice to clients' (quoted in *Social Work Today*, 23 April 1984, p.9). The second point in the BASW resolution recalls the discussion in Chapter 5 on information systems. For our present purposes, though, the important question is : how far will such declarations by BASW find an echo within training course planning machinery?

CCETSW had indeed already begun to make moves on the question of more adequate training in welfare benefits matters. In 1982 research was conducted by John Jacobs, at Sussex University, into the use made on social work courses of training materials relating to supplementary benefit. This research was commissioned by a joint working group set up by DHSS and the Social Work and Social Administration Committees of the Joint University Council. Chaired by the Assistant Director of CCETSW, this group responded to Jacobs's findings by setting up CCETSW-supported workshops in March 1983 and September 1984, bringing together DHSS staff and social work teachers to discuss how progress might be made. Jacobs had concluded that 'welfare rights are a crucial element in social work teaching on a few courses, but in many more they are only marginal' (quoted in *Community Care*, 2 August 1984, p.13). The March 1983 workshop, according to *Community Care*, identified the following elements necessary to an effort to remedy such a shortfall:

> More opportunities to be made available for student placements in supplementary benefits offices. For many years only about 500 of the 3500 students joining social work courses each year have done a one-week practice placement in a supplementary benefit office. More study opportunities for social work teachers in supplementary benefit offices should be provided. Currently available teaching aids on supplementary benefit and welfare rights from DHSS, CAB, courses etc. should be identified and included in a directory which might also include demonstration tapes of interviews held at DHSS regional training centres. A film for students should be produced.

These initiatives were cited by CCETSW's Assistant Director, Reg Wright, in a letter to BASW responding to the above resolution. He also observed that 'well over 100 teachers of social work and social policy have...taken up the opportunity...to spend a period in a local or regional [DHSS] office'; and pointed to the importance of discussing the legitimacy of welfare rights teaching on social work courses, as 'not everyone accepted it was part of social work' (quoted in 'BASW News', *Social Work Today*, 6 August 1984).

Such developments are indeed encouraging and one looks forward to firm progress in the future. I feel, though, that one note of caution is required. The current CCETSW interest in this area does seem to be heavily dependent on the DHSS and to be taking place more or less in isolation from local authority welfare rights interests. This may be remedied as training initiatives begin to take a more developed form, but for example at the meeting on 8 June 1984 of the national Welfare Rights Officers Group, which predominantly represents LA welfare rights advisers from all over Britain, few delegates had heard of the CCETSW-supported initiatives described above, and none had done so in his or her official local authority capacity as such. That the DHSS has a valuable contribution to make to such developments is clear : but to rely excessively on the main benefit-administering agency itself is to court the danger that liaison will be (rightly) stressed but advocacy (disastrously) neglected, while DHSS perspectives crowd out a more client-orientated approach. This could lead to social workers' welfare rights role appearing from the outside as a rather toothless beast, which would do little for the credibility of the profession or the interests of clients. There is a pressing need for a healthy injection of welfare rights experience into current deliberations on course planning.

However good, or otherwise, a professional course may be in preparing a social worker for applying welfare rights skills in practice, there will be serious limitations on the 'life' of the knowledge. Some skills, such as in negotiating techniques, will be of lasting value (although even they can be overtaken by major changes of legal structure); but the detailed information dates rapidly. Social security systems have long been subject to changes in the law, policy and practice : but we have seen that since 1979, the tempo of change has been stepped up. Major pieces of legislation have been frequent; more detailed changes almost continuous; while changes of policy, substantial and minor, follow in profusion. It is apparent, then, that the professional course can give only a grounding. Good, regular in-service training is crucial if an acceptable standard of practice is to be maintained.

In-service training

The role of a local welfare rights resource in providing and maintaining information systems is reflected in the training sphere also. Such a body will be ideally placed to monitor training needs and to liaise with departmental training sections, area offices and other relevant interests to organise training programmes and packages tailored to local requirements.

We must, however, deal first with the world as it is, and there will be many social services agencies which will not have the advantage of such a local resource with which to work. In such cases, the agencies concerned will have to improvise, making the best use of whatever facilities are available. Local universities, polytechnics and colleges may well be able to help. One option which I shall look at in some degree of detail is that of 'buying in' expertise which may be available elsewhere in the region, or even nationally.

It is unlikely that a social services agency will be able to release enough staff time to permit the *ideal* level of in-service training, even if such training could otherwise be provided on the necessary scale. The aim should therefore be to provide at least a fairly thorough session – perhaps half a day – at reasonably frequent intervals. Exact feasible levels will depend on local pressures of other work, but if staff are not receiving at least a thorough annual refresher session, then they are likely to be showing marked signs of rust as far as welfare rights knowledge is concerned. A well-designed induction course, for new staff, will also include a significant welfare rights component.

The precise level and nature of in-service training which is required will vary to some extent depending on the local picture not only in terms of caseload content, but also of the availability of other sources of welfare rights advice, both for social services staff and for clients. For example, a good local advice centre will permit responsible referring-on of some more complicated cases (*not*, one hastens to add, the instant unloading of any case requiring a legal reference or a calculator). Availability of welfare rights advice by telephone will also assist day-to-day practice in the area office. Many staff will, however, have nothing to fall back on but their own resources. This will help to determine the necessary scale, scope of coverage and detail of any training programme.

Training concerning *strategy and tactics* is also important. Knowing that somebody is entitled to a benefit is one thing; making sure that he or she gets (or keeps) it is another. This is particularly important in relation to the unemployed and to single parents, the two groups of claimants most likely to experience aggressive 'claims control' tactics; and who have suffered long years of negative stereotyping in the mass media, which may lead to unofficial 'discouragement' by benefit clerks – all of this exacerbated by the effects of DHSS staff shortages on local office practices (see for example Moore, 1980; McKnight, 1985; Smith, 1985). Negotiating style, familiarity with some of the more 'unofficial' practices and general 'know-how' are important here. This recalls Becker's point, above, concerning training for advocacy.

Much of the above applies to training for professional qualifications also, but an in-service course can draw upon the specific local context to provide valuable detail and immediacy. This returns us to the question of what welfare rights teaching resources are available locally. When planning an in-service course or session, sensitivity to the right choice of teacher(s) is essential. Detailed knowledge of the technicalities of the subject is required; but, precisely because the subject is so technical, so is a good, 'communicating' teaching style. Some reasonably close connection with welfare rights work in the field will also be necessary if the 'street wisdom' discussed above is to be brought to bear. If the social services agency has access to its own welfare rights resource, then presumably these problems will be taken care of. If not, additional attention to detail will be called for from the agency itself. In all cases, course organisers at every level should seek feedback from course attenders, even where a welfare rights body has been commissioned to handle the training : such organisations tend to have a reputation for high levels of expertise, which is usually deserved, but there can be exceptions, especially where short-term funding and/or low pay lead to problems of high staff turnover; or where volunteers are inadequately trained. A good course organiser will have a 'nose' for such matters.

If such resources are simply not available within the locality, it may be possible, as noted above, to look further afield, perhaps to a nearby area where courses are available. Alternatively, it may be possible to negotiate an affordable training deal with a national body such as CPAG. The latter has developed a well-established service along these lines, so I shall use it as an example.

The central element in CPAG's training efforts is its intensive week-long course, held bi-monthly and for some time an important component of national welfare rights training resources. Social services agencies constitute one of the course's 'best customers', although of course the cost implications are very different depending on the agency's proximity to Central London. It will in any case be helpful to give some details of course content, as an illustration of the sorts of issues which have proved the most useful to course attenders over the years. The following is based on a 1984 course programme (I am grateful to Alan Booth for details):

Monday
1 The structure of the social security system
2 Supplementary benefit – introduction to the scheme; who can claim; cohabitation; conditions of entitlement; the basic calculation
3 Supplementary benefit – single payments
4 Preparing and presenting supplementary benefit appeals – including mock tribunals

Tuesday
1 Supplementary benefit – normal and additional requirements; resources
2 Housing benefit – standard cases; housing benefit supplement
3 Housing benefit – certificated cases; reviews; housing costs for people on supplementary benefit
4 Family income supplement and the poverty trap; housing benefit (poverty trap effects); education benefits; free

prescriptions, dental and optical treatment; free welfare foods and milk; their combined effects
5 Preparing mock tribunals – supplementary benefit (SB) appeal (alleged self-deprivation of resources); SB appeal (refusal of single payment); SB appeal (alleged cohabitation); unemployment benefit appeal (alleged voluntary unemployment)

Wednesday
1 Fuel – fuel debts; threat of disconnection; DHSS liaison with fuel boards
2 National Insurance – unemployment and retirement
3 Tax – an introduction to the tax system; how to calculate a family's bill; the pay-as-you-earn system; common law families; the treatment of maintenance; taxation of benefits
4 Mock tribunal (single payments)
5 Negotiations with the DHSS – emergencies and common problems concerning supplementary benefit

Thursday
1 National Insurance – administration; appeals and reviews; 'due care and diligence'; good cause for late claim; preparing an appeal
2 Mock tribunal (alleged cohabitation)
3 Industrial injuries – benefits in respect of
4 Benefits for disabled people – attendance allowance; mobility allowance; severe disablement allowance
5 Mock tribunal (alleged voluntary unemployment)
6 Statutory sick pay
7 Child benefit
8 Fraud

Friday
1 A practical exercise summarising the week's work
2 Mock tribunal
3 The role of CPAG

All sessions include practical exercises.

The first thing to spring to mind from the above is that it is very hard work! Indeed, such rapid and intensive treatment of some very complicated areas of benefit provision can only be seen as laying a foundation. Following this up with periodic refresher training and more extensive treatment of particular areas will be essential.

CPAG does indeed provide additional one-day courses and seminars, again based in London. Moreover, it is possible to negotiate half-day, one-day and two-day courses 'made to measure' to the customer's requirements and based in the customer's locality. As the CPAG publicity leaflet puts it:

> We've no preference for Shoreham, Shoreditch, Swansea or Strathclyde. We are equipped to respond to most circumstances. Among the groups taking part in the past twelve months have been housing departments, careers specialists, lawyers, student service officers, social workers, health visitors, estate management staff and medical social workers. (Child Poverty Action Group, 1984)

This same leaflet, incidentally, reminds us that, while a variety of different types of agency may provide welfare rights training, those which themselves have day-to-day dealings with welfare rights problems enjoy certain advantages:

> Our daily contact with the problems and issues as they arise in the social security system is crucial to our ability to provide sucessful training courses for so many varied groups and interests. Every year our Citizens' Rights Office deals with over 5000 enquiries from claimants, social workers, advice centres etc. on virtually every aspect of the provision of welfare benefits. This cumulative experience, besides helping thousands of people each year, provides an invaluable resource from which we draw in our teaching programme.

While CPAG operates the most developed welfare rights training resource of this sort at a national level, it is not the only agency with a training capacity in the welfare rights field. For example, the Institute of Housing was very active in providing training sessions in various parts of the country on the introduction of the housing benefit scheme in 1982 – 3.

An example of a regional training resource is the joint training programme operated on Tyneside by Newcastle Welfare Rights Service and Tyneside Housing Aid Centre. Although these bodies have a Newcastle and Tyneside focus respectively, their joint training facilities are in fact subscribed to by agencies from all over the Northern Region and sometimes beyond. Again, an intensive week-long course is the central pivot, with a variety of additional seminars and short courses designed to meet particular needs. To put, once more, some flesh on the bones of this description, the following outline programme for mid-1984/85 may be of interest to the reader. It was drawn up by the (then) training organisers of the two agencies, Lynne Caffrey and Sheila Spencer, and illustrates current concerns in the benefit field which had given rise to a perceived need for training:

Week-Long Course: Joint housing and welfare rights course no.12 – there is already a waiting list for this course; there is a commitment to run three of these courses each year and we would recommend that this continues.

Two-Day Packages (Supplementary Benefit; Housing Benefit): With the recent changes in the housing benefit scheme and the continuing complexities of the supplementary benefit scheme it has become apparent that this type of course will have appeal and be of benefit to a wide range of people. It is recommended that two initial two-day courses are arranged with a view to running more if demand is shown.

Half-Day Courses (Housing Benefit – Reviews and Review Boards): Given the scarcity of information available on the review system and the lack of use to which it is put, there is an obvious need to run a series of half-day courses. These would be advertised very widely and an initial two would be organised to assess demand.

One-Day Courses ('Equal Treatment' between Men and Women within Social Security): Following a very successful one-day course in June, it is recommended that a further two courses are organised.

One-Day Courses (Appeal Tribunals – New Adjudication Procedures): A lot of advisers are very unsure about the implications and effects of the new adjudication system. It is recommended that two, day-long courses are arranged to explain how the new system affects the appeal procedure, and how to prepare an appeal.

One-Day Courses (Supplementary Benefit – Single People either Homeless or Setting-up Home for the First Time): Given the special range of problems which this group of people suffers, especially in relation to the 'suitable alternative furnished accommodation' rules, it is recommended that two, day-long courses are arranged, with a view to running more if demand is shown. It will be important to co-ordinate work on these courses with Single Homeless on Tyneside and other rights agencies concerned with homelessness-related issues.

In-Service Training Sessions for Welfare Rights Workers : It is recommended that meetings are arranged with relevant advice agencies to plan the next in-service training programme.

Thus, considerable possibilities may exist at national or regional levels for social services agencies to 'plug into' existing training programmes or to commission courses from established welfare rights bodies. But even so, the strictly locally-provided welfare rights training facility will, as long as the capacity genuinely exists in the area, inevitably enjoy certain adventages. It is true that most legislation is indeed national in focus in the social security field, albeit usually locally administered. Nevertheless, there are, firstly, certain exceptions, notably in relation to benefits and services administered by the SSD and the education department; there are also areas of discretion within national frameworks, for example in the housing benefit field. However, perhaps the most important aspect of 'local knowledge' is the detailed experience of how this or that social security office or fuel board actually operates in practice; how the system functions 'on the ground' in that particular area.

Moreover, there is more to effective welfare rights work than a knowledge of benefits, their administration and relevant advocacy techniques. For example there will from time to time be a need to refer a case on to another agency, perhaps to take advantage of a particular specialism, or because it is unusually difficult, calling for more intensive treatment. Here, a good knowledge of various services locally available, and of relevant referral procedures, will be required.

I would like to enlarge a little on the question of referral procedures, for the lack of attention to what should really be a straightforward issue, in practice causes a good deal of frustration, inconvenience and even hardship to clients. Responsible referral procedures should be applied whatever the agency to which the client is being referred. Advice centres raise special problems, though, as they (along with certain other bodies – doctors' surgeries being an obvious example) will frequently operate sessions at specified times, the centre being closed and perhaps nobody being present at other times. The most common form of sloppy referral is to send a client to an advice session without bothering to look up session times. Thus, social security claimants who can ill afford wasted bus fares or additional aggravation may be sent on expensive and frustrating wild goose chases around the town. A knowledge of local facilities *and how to use them*, including referral procedures and the use of appointment systems where available, should be part of local training programmes and information systems.

A locally-organised training programme is, then, in a good position to develop knowledge and skills over a wide spectrum, from the intricacies of a supplementary or housing benefit calculation to the range of local services available and how to use them. 'Buying in' expertise from other parts of the country may be fine as a useful supplement to the in-house or other local training capacity, but if it has to be done as a desperate measure in the absence of more accessible facilities, then something is wrong with the local training resources. In the worst instances, even minimal levels of in-service training will simply not take place at all: and too often, one suspects that this is the case.

7

Taking-up Wider Issues

Social workers, WROs, day centre staff and indeed anybody who seeks to advise or assist people on low incomes will find that the same problems arise again and again in different cases. It seems to me to be very difficult to work in any close proximity to welfare rights issues without noticing that our income maintenance systems are as much part of the problem as part of the solution. The difficulties of poor people can be traced not only to unemployment, disability or some other adverse life circumstance, but to the operation of social security and welfare benefit systems themselves:

● Not only has Mr Jones been dismissed from his job, following an argument which he feels was provoked by his employer, but the employer says that Mr Jones left voluntarily, and the adjudication officer believes him. Mr Jones has therefore had his unemployment benefit stopped for six weeks.

● Not only has Mr Green been forced to take part-time work, after losing his full-time job and not being able to find another, but the adjudication officer says that three days a week is now the 'full extent' of his 'normal' work pattern, and has stopped his unemployment benefit for the days on which he does not work.

● Ms Jenkins, a single parent, has had her supplementary benefit stopped, because the adjudication officer says she is still living with her husband: she is not, but she may now have to allow him to return, even though he has this unfortunate habit of beating her up.

● The Philipsons are elderly private tenants and the good news is that they are entitled to a substantial amount of housing benefit: the bad news is that the local authority has not paid it and they are in considerable rent arrears. When they finally do get it, it will be minus the housing benefit supplement which nobody realises they are entitled to.

These cases are distilled from numerous such instances which I and my colleagues have encountered regularly over the years. Many more examples of similar problems with this or that benefit or group of claimants could be cited. Many readers, and any advice centre, will find such a sorry catalogue only too familiar. The point I wish to make here, though, is that welfare rights problems seem to cry out for solutions which go beyond the individual case to tackle features of the income maintenance system itself which are causing or exacerbating claimants' problems.

Within this perspective, there are various different levels of intervention. One approach might be to try to make existing provisions work better: for example, the repeated encountering of unclaimed supplementary benefit amongst unemployed clients may suggest a take-up campaign aimed at the clientele of the local unemployment benefit office. Another approach may be to seek to change local authority policies : for example, the Education Department may have a clothing grant scheme which does not extend to children of people involved in trade disputes, perhaps on the grounds that such circumstances are temporary. Thus, much hardship may remain untreated during lengthy disputes. Such schemes are discretionary: so lobbying of councillors on the Education Committee may well secure an improvement. A further approach might be to seek to change the practice of the local DHSS office : for example, habitually cursory examination of possible entitlement to supplementary benefit additional requirements – say, for special diets or extra laundry costs – might be scrutinised, publicised and practice ultimately improved.

It is possible also to aim one's efforts at changes to the legislation. This idea usually seems very remote and unrealistic to practitioners 'in the field', and indeed one does not expect readily to secure major changes in government social and economic policies. However, gains can be made or setbacks resisted. For example, when I worked on Newcastle Welfare Rights Service's first advice session, in the mid-1970s, one of the most obvious injustices of the then rent allowance system seemed to me to be the 'furniture deduction', where furnished tenants in effect had their benefit reduced to reflect the value of their furniture. The theory was that, if they did not wish to purchase this 'service' (that is, the 'enjoyment' of the furniture) they could always move into unfurnished accommodation and buy their own. Quite apart, then, from the rather surprising weekly amounts which could be ascribed to the value of the old junk with which some private landlords kitted out their flats, the whole policy was underpinned by a view of tenure patterns and disposable incomes that can only be described as a confused nonsense, completely out of touch with social reality. The result was a clearly visible injustice to claimants. Thus, some years later when I was a member of the Association of Metropolitan Authorities' team at the talks concerning the introduction of the now notorious housing benefit scheme, one of my first objectives was to enlist the support of the local authority associations in getting rid of the 'furniture deduction'. (The pursuit of larger-scale local authority association objectives, such as an adequately-financed housing benefit scheme, unfortunately proved rather less fruitful.)

I am not, of course, suggesting that readers will regularly find opportunities to enter into direct discussions with central government ; but there are channels whereby contacts can be made with those who are frequently thus engaged: the local authority associations are just one example – they and others are further discussed below, as we move on to consider in more detail the question of strategy and tactics.

Strategy and tactics

The considerations which surround attempts to influence local authority policies have already been discussed in Chapter 4, in the context of efforts to persuade LAs to set up welfare rights resources. I shall not repeat the arguments here. The local offices of the central benefit-administering machinery will present their own problems and possibilities. In some matters of policy and practice, they will prove inflexible, pursuing a centrally-determined line; but local

DHSS managers in many respects have considerable autonomy and may be persuaded to revise working practices, within the obvious limitations of the benefit legislation and the administrative resources available to them.

There will be common ground with the DHSS trade unions over a range of 'quality of service' issues, notably but not exclusively staffing levels, so it is well worth establishing contacts here. In some areas this has extended as far as joint demonstrations of DHSS staff, welfare rights workers and claimants' representatives against arbitrary and aggressive 'anti-fraud' measures. In Newcastle, a leaked internal document, written in 1983 by a 'specialist claims control' (SCC) team leader, reported that the 'normal success rate' of his team had been 'prejudiced' by such activity. He complained of 'adverse publicity instigated by Trade Unions and Welfare Rights organisations. This was aggravated to such an extent that leaflets were being distributed outside the office to all the claimants visiting there. That action was continued for about a fortnight'. (It should be noted that 'success' by SCC criteria is measured largely in terms of claims which are withdrawn as a result of the activity of SCC squads. One view, to be found, significantly, amongst both rights workers and DHSS staff, is that intimidation by SCC tactics, rather than fear arising from a fraudulent claim, is frequently the factor at work here. See Smith, 1985, for a discussion of this and other causes for concern with regard to SCC.)

Particularly at a local level, it will often be possible to form alliances with claimants' own organisations – for example, tenants' associations or claimants' unions. This can lead to energetic grassroots campaigns into which claimants' own participation injects a crucial element of first-hand experience and knowledge.

Where central government is concerned, the most fruitful method may be to talk to the chairperson of an appropriate LA committee concerning possible approaches which might be made to bodies such as the AMA, Association of County Councils, Association of District Councils or Convention of Scottish Local Authorities. Similarly, the relevant chief officers' group may be prepared to pursue issues which are of interest to them: the Association of Directors of Social Services and (in Scotland) the Association of Directors of Social Work have both proved ready to take up welfare rights questions.

Alternatively, it may be appropriate to enlist the interest and support of pressure groups such as CPAG, Shelter, the Disability Alliance, Disablement Income Group, Low Pay Unit, National Council for One Parent Families, and so on. Political parties, trade unions and professional bodies such as BASW may all provide useful channels of pressure and influence.

A key consideration at all levels will of course be the most effective style of campaigning/lobbying and degree of militancy associated with the pursuit of wider welfare rights issues. Whether demonstrations, pickets, mass media coverage, formal meetings or discreet lobbying, or any combination of them, hold out the best prospects of success, will depend on the issue and the degree of receptiveness of the 'target' body. Agencies and individuals will vary in the extent to which they feel able to adopt the more controversial styles of campaigning.

Take-up campaigns also raise important questions of strategy and methods. Large-scale 'blitzes' such as the 1980 Strathclyde 'postcard campaign' described in Chapter 4 are now likely to be relatively less productive, given recent legislative changes, than targeted efforts such as those described below and in Chapter 2. There are also substantial opportunities presented by modern computer technology : for example, LAs' housing benefit records hold out considerable prospects for targeted, computerised take-up exercises if the political will can be generated to launch this sort of initiative.

There is much which could be said concerning the details of appropriate strategies and tactics and it is not possible to do the subject justice in a brief treatment here. I hope, though, that the illustrations given later in this chapter will convey an impression of some of the processes at work in real-life attempts to generalise from individual problems and tackle wider issues. I would like to consider first, though, some of the factors which will influence the extent to which an individual is likely to wish to, or indeed be able to pursue such wider problems, moving along the advocacy continuum to embrace unequivocally 'cause' advocacy. I would like to focus here not on WROs or community workers, who are likely to engage in such work as a clearly recognised part of their job, but on social workers, who provide a prominent example of a professional group still hesitating on the edge of uncharted, and moreover muddy waters in this respect. There are two major aspects to this discussion : that of individual philosophies and attitudes; and that of agency philosophy, priorities and organisation.

The individual

The question of individual attitudes to welfare rights within social work was considered in some detail in Chapter 2. Here, though, we are concerned with the specific question of individual attitudes towards the pursuit of welfare rights advocacy to the level of cause advocacy. Here again there are — as we shall see below — both 'prescriptive' and *'laissez-faire'* schools of thought as to whether social workers *must* embrace advocacy at this level, or whether it is in fact legitimate for them to exercise a choice as to how far and on what scale they, personally, should pursue an issue. I argued in Chapter 2 that, given certain conditions, there is scope 'for individual social workers to choose the speed and braking power with which they proceed along the advocacy continuum'. Nevertheless, my hope is that as many social workers as possible will be attracted to the idea of cause advocacy in their clients' interests.

The personal philosophy of the individual, in relation both to welfare rights and to social action, will be a major factor in determining degree of motivation and the way in which the value of such work is perceived. It can be argued that welfare rights work is not necessarily a radical activity and conservative interpretations of it can, in theory at least, be developed: I touched on some of these myself in Chapter 4 and indeed argued that it was necessary to know more about them if poor people in large areas of the country were not to continue to lack welfare rights provision. My own view is nevertheless somewhat different : from my personal perspective, I see the concept of welfare rights as having definitely socialist implications. Briefly, this is because of its dual emphases, on the one hand on the rights of the individual *vis-a-vis* the bureaucracy; and on the other, on the responsibility of society to make collective provision for the needs of its members. I argued in Chapter 1 that the welfare rights approach is not exclusively concerned with poverty, having a continuing interest in individual rights and the distribution of power and resources which would persist even in the absence of extremes of inequality and deprivation. It would thus not be expected to wither away in the absence of capitalism, as some more romantically inclined WROs suppose. This interpretation of course has nothing to do with paternalistic and bureaucratic perceptions of 'socialism', where the concept of individual welfare (or indeed other) rights may be equated with undesirable boat-rocking and ingratitude for what has been provided; but it has everything to do with socialism as I interpret it: the right of an individual to flourish within a context of social responsibility and collective provision for need, the latter being indeed a necessary condition if all individuals *are* to have the right to develop their potential.

It is, though, not necessary to invoke a personal philosophical stance of this sort in order to argue that social services staff can or should be involved in 'cause' advocacy. It is true that, almost by definition, work aimed at altering the status quo in some respect will not sit easily with strictly conservative notions : but almost any perspective which regards some concept of reform, however mild, as legitimate, will potentially have a place for cause advocacy within its range of possible methods. Thus, the advocacy of causes, rather than merely individual cases, can be regarded as an integral part of social work, rather than purely a private matter for the individual. Some social workers will indeed argue that cause advocacy is a professional duty. A good illustration of this approach was provided in the following correspondence in the social work press in 1984. Commenting on one of Tony Bennett's typically forthright statements (1984b, p.16) on the 'social worker's responsibility to give sound practical help to clients to claim their benefits and assert their rights', a reader from Hackney SSD urges that, while Bennett's argument is

> both forceful and convincing...the matter cannot possibly rest there. Faced with an increasing number of clients whose problems are not only exacerbated, but actually multiplied, and in some cases even *caused* by the Kafkaesque world of 'social security', social workers have a *twofold* duty : not only...*direct* work with (and alongside) clients...but also *indirect* work in the form of pressure on individual DHSS officers, offices as a whole, and ultimately government itself, to acknowledge *their* duty to positively provide for citizens' social security needs...This is not an argument for 'political' action over and above the 'professional' sphere; it pertains to a 'unitary approach'...that is firmly rooted in the social work task itself...This sort of approach to social security should be taken up in the theory and practice of the social work profession as a whole. (Slater, 1984, p.3)

Similarly, Stuart Etherington (at the time, BASW's professional officer for policy) has argued (1984, p.15) that :

> The relationship between advocacy and social reform is a close one. At what point for example does the establishment of groups who argue for take-up campaigns become social action rather than advocacy? The dividing line is thin. Social workers must not shirk the responsibility they have to initiate social reform and social action. The establishment of centres for unemployed people and other groups will encourage some form of cohesiveness upon which action can be based.

It is hard to say how far such attitudes are widespread within the social work profession; and how much weight we should attach to reports such as the following (from a news item in *Community Care*, 19 January 1984, on a 1984 International Federation of Social Workers seminar) that: 'Social workers believe they should promote social action and client participation rather than encourage clients to accept poverty, according to conclusions drawn at an EEC-funded seminar on responding to poverty.' However, such rumblings are encouraging if one takes the view that there is more to social work than mopping up the individual casualties.

The perspectives of the individual are, though, only part of the story. Just as social workers will not have the time or the resources to tackle welfare rights problems at the individual level unless the agency itself sees this as a legitimate activity, similarly – and perhaps to an even greater extent – effective cause advocacy will require agency endorsement and support.

The agency

Olive Stevenson (1973, p.202) has described the growing 'poverty lobby' activity of the early 1970s as leading to 'a more articulate and militant strategy amongst some social workers in their relationship to government, be it local or central. The dilemmas this poses for the professional within a bureaucracy are well known and much discussed'.

The problems which may arise are not confined to possible conflict between the 'social action' orientation of some individual social workers and more traditionally bureaucratic or perhaps actively unsympathetic management. It may be that management simply does not accord a high priority to this sort of work and therefore does not make time and other resources available, sufficiently or at all. The traditional 'one-to-one' casework approach to social work will indeed tend to give rise to this sort of obstacle.

Thus, it seemed to me in the late 1970s that the situation described by Stevenson had not developed within social work to any very large extent; and I found myself arguing in the social work press that, as regards involvement in efforts to tackle problems by influencing central or local government policies, this was much less likely to arise amongst social workers than amongst community or rights workers.

> The problem is frequently not one of lack of interest, but of the transition from concern to action, and here the organisational context of social work is an obstacle. Social work is still largely geared to the individual case, and while the links between many such individual problems and aspects of social and economic

policies are obvious to many social workers, it is not so clear to them what they can do about it. Other fieldworkers are more likely to be expected to approach problems on several different levels *as part of their job*. (Fimister, 1979a, p.17)

Individual attitudes and agency expectations do of course overlap and interact, the latter perhaps tending to influence the former rather more than vice versa. Thus a professional outlook which, often partly as a result of the emphases of much social work training, tends towards 'individualisation' of clients' problems, will be further encouraged by the terms in which the agency defines 'the job'. Those who have other ideas will meanwhile come under institutional pressure, perhaps subtle rather than overt, to conform to the prevailing model. Caroline Watts, a senior social worker from Birmingham, describes (1981) the influence of orthodox professional attitudes thus : 'Social workers can and should consider themselves as potential agents of social change and should recognise that they can have some political influence. Unfortunately, our individual approach to problem solving makes us hesitant to tackle wider issues.' She goes on to ask how many social workers will have submitted evidence to the supplementary benefit review of the late 1970s; and how many seek to pursue their clients' interests through their trade unions. Moreover, social workers neglect

> the possibilities of working with claimants as a group. On a very simple level, while we may fight hard to get an extra heating addition for a claimant whose flat is damp, we never think to extend this to the other occupants of the block, or of other blocks built to the same design. (Watts, 1981)

(She would, I am sure, approve very much of the 'McCutcheons Court' case study described below, which pursued this very issue.)

I shall go on now to devote the rest of this chapter to giving illustrations of and ideas for action to take up wider issues, encompassing three major dimensions of this question: lobbying the policy-makers; joint action with claimants; and the 'hearts and minds' problem – how to combat anti-welfare ideology in order to build up public and political support for policies to combat poverty and improve social security.

Lobbying the policy-makers

The example I would like to take here is the long-running saga of overlapping responsibilities of DHSS and SSDs for making lump-sum payments to claimants/clients in certain circumstances; and the involvement of Newcastle SSD in seeking to influence DHSS practice and policies and to develop a firm policy on the part of the Newcastle Social Services Committee. This example is interesting, not so much because it leads to any clearly defined success (indeed, the saga still continues and no early resolution of the problem is expected), but because it illustrates the wide range of channels which have proved to be required.

I do not propose to repeat here the various arguments which surround this issue, but a brief summary is called for. In England and Wales, the problem has largely been discussed in terms of Section 1 of the 1980 Child Care Act (formerly Section 1 of the Children and Young Persons Act 1963) which provides SSDs with powers to make cash payments in certain circumstances – that is, in order to seek to prevent a child from being received into or remaining in public care or appearing before a juvenile court (see for example Emett and Lister, 1976; Lister, 1977; Fimister, 1977, 1979c and 1980b; Hill and Laing, 1978; Department of Health and Social Security, 1979). In Scotland, Section 12 of the Social Work (Scotland) Act 1968 confers broadly analogous powers (Campbell, 1977). The role of social workers in making such payments is, amongst others, one akin to benefit administration rather than to welfare rights advocacy; but contentious welfare rights issues, which have given rise to much case and cause advocacy, surround this question. To cut a long story short, it is widely felt within SSDs and elsewhere that these powers are often seen by the DHSS as an excuse for evading its own responsibilities in relation to lump-sum payments under the single payments and/or urgent cases provisions of the supplementary benefit legislation. Obviously, this has implications for the budgets of SSDs which the latter are not going to like: but does it matter from the claimant's point of view, as long as somebody pays? The answer, I think, is that yes, it does, for the following reasons : it prevents the operation of a clear and dignified claiming process; it furthers a drift away from a central social security system of entitlements, including appeal rights, and towards localised discretionary handouts; it erodes SSD 'Section 1' and analogous budgets to the detriment of clients not entitled to DHSS payments; and where confusion exists, one likely result will be that nobody exercises responsibility. Social workers also argue that the use of 'Section 1'-type funds for legitimate social work objectives is thwarted by this process. The problem, it should be noted, has two main variants : the use of SSD funds to pay for day-to-day necessities such as clothing, which should more properly be the province of the supplementary benefit scheme; and the provision of emergency funds, for example when benefit girocheques fail to turn up, in the absence of an adequate urgent payments system at DHSS. Restrictions placed on DHSS payments in 1980, and radical cuts and structural change (the 'social fund') being proposed at the time of writing, have further inflamed the issue.

This problem was identified as a cause for concern by social workers, the Welfare Rights Service and SSD management in Newcastle in the mid-1970s and has been taken up in various different ways since then : proposals to the Social Services Committee; publicity locally, regionally and nationally; representations to the DHSS, to the Supplementary Benefit Review in the late 1970s and to the Social Security Advisory Committee (SSAC) – this last effort by means of collaboration with the CPAG; the pursuit of improved local liaison machinery with the DHSS; and most recently, an unexpected exchange with the Social Security Minister over the tentative suggestion that social workers might become more involved in benefit administration. I shall now look at these different aspects of this lobbying and campaigning process in more detail.

A firm committee policy

In 1976, Brian Roycroft, Newcastle SSD's Director,

convened a working party consisting of himself, two members of the social work staff from different area teams, and myself as welfare rights team leader. The purpose was to formulate guidelines to put to the Social Services Committee concerning the handling of this troublesome 'frontier problem' (a term originated by David Donnison, then Chairman of the Supplementary Benefits Commission). It was felt that the subject was important enough to merit a specific decision by elected members. The subsequent Committee report, which I was asked to draft on the basis of the working party's findings, benefited considerably from a 'social work angle' on a question which I had seen in the past largely in 'welfare rights' terms : that is, I had emphasised the points made above concerning the need for a clear claiming process and the proper role of social security. But the working party also stressed the need for such funds to be used, in the Director's phrase, 'as part of a creative social work strategy to promote the wellbeing of children' (quoted in Fimister, 1977, p.3). An example would be the payment of child care costs to enable a single parent to go out to work and escape from supplementary benefit. The report, in its proposed procedures, insisted on the necessity to press DHSS for payment before 'Section 1' funds were considered, the possibility of an appeal being carefully investigated where necessary. DHSS should be pressed to reimburse the SSD for payments made on an urgent basis, and 'Section 1' loans could be made where cases were being appealed, to be repaid in the event of the appeal proving successful.

The Social Services Committee adopted this report on 11 November 1976. It cannot be said that its provisions are always consistently applied across the SSD, but it certainly raised the profile of the issue and attracted a fair degree of attention. Ruth Lister (1977, pp.10—11), in an open letter to the Chairman of the Supplementary Benefits Commission, commented that:

> Social Services Departments seeking more helpful guidance [that is, more helpful than the official liaison guidelines] could well take a look at a policy statement recently approved by Newcastle Social Services Committee...clear guidelines for

dealing with the Supplementary Benefits Commission on the lines adopted by Newcastle must be drawn up. Then and only then can one claim that the SSD/social security frontier problem is being tackled effectively.

Publicity and representations to the DHSS and the Social Security Advisory Committee

Demand for copies of the Newcastle Committee report proved substantial, so the Welfare Rights Service wrote a commentary around it and issued it as a published report (Fimister, 1977). It was widely circulated to social services interests around the country and submitted to the DHSS at local, regional and national levels. In 1979, as a spin-off from the Supplementary Benefit Review, the DHSS published a report on 'relations with social services' (DHSS, 1979) and proceeded to consult with LA interests. This was used by the Welfare Rights Service once more as an opportunity to publicise, amongst other things, the 'Section 1' issue : a report was produced (Fimister, 1979c) and given the same sort of publicity and circulation as its predecessor. In 1980, the CPAG produced, in pamphlet form, an open letter to the newly-established SSAC: acting as both a CPAG National Executive Committee member and as LA welfare rights adviser, I contributed a chapter on 'frontier problems' (Fimister, 1980b), which amongst other things again took up the 'Section 1' question, this time in the context of the new legal basis of the supplementary benefit system.

All of this contributed to a wider questioning, by a number of commentators, of the dubious role of supplementary benefit policy and practice in this area : but one hopes that the sustained Newcastle effort, especially within the social services professional networks, may have had some concrete effect on the terms of the debate and on social workers' resolve 'on the ground' (if not on subsequent legislation – which has worsened the problem by making supplementary benefit single payments harder to obtain).

Local liaison machinery

In 1984, Newcastle's Welfare Rights/Social Work Liaison Group (constructed from the welfare rights information distribution network – see Chapter 5) set up a working party to look once more at the 'frontiers' question. As one consequence of this, I subsequently conducted a small-scale survey of problems which social work teams were having with emergency payments. The picture which emerged from this was so fragmented and variable that it seemed that there was a good case for at least trying to clear the lines of communication between local DHSS offices and SSD area teams : this could possibly be of use where the DHSS was resisting emergency payments and the appeal process was regarded as inappropriate, because of the time-lag involved and because the size of the sum in question did not justify the 'make a loan and pursue an appeal' technique.

One promising 'angle' on this was the 'working practices group' recently set up in West Newcastle. Such groups are a current manifestation of more 'consumer-orientated' trends within the DHSS, and the West Newcastle case has, at the time of writing, yet to spread to other parts of the City. The local WRO reports that : 'The Group comprises officers of the DHSS, advice and social workers. Meetings are held on a quarterly basis...Discussion is open and critical, and, judging from the DHSS report back on the first meeting, positive' (Wellburn, 1984). For our present purposes, the most relevant outcome of this exercise has been a DHSS decision to set up a separate section for single payments. WROs in East Newcastle have been pursuing similar liaison facilities, and the Central/North DHSS office has been making limited consumer-orientated overtures which may lead in the same direction. It should be stressed that such arrangements are far more comprehensive than the 'liaison officer' machinery; and provided that they are seen as foci for hard-headed negotiation rather than amicable coffee afternoons, could provide a real opportunity to sort out at least some local difficulties.

Social workers and benefit assessments

Newcastle's most recent contribution to the 'frontiers' debate arose unexpectedly during the AMA's oral evidence to the 1984 Supplementary Benefit Review, which I presented alongside Toby Harris, current Vice-Chairman of the AMA Social Services Committee. The hearing had been largely predictable, the AMA team turning the discussion as often as possible to its main preoccupations – inadequate benefit levels; blinkered scope of the Review terms of reference; grossly inadequate staffing levels in the DHSS – when the Minister, Tony Newton, posed an unexpected question:

> Assuming that there does seem to be some fairly widespread support for extending the area of discretion a bit from what it is at present, even if not going back as far as the position before 1980, how would you see the role of the local authorities...in any such change if such were to take place?...If there were to be a greater discretionary element in the scheme, that would involve what amounts to in some respects a social work kind of assessment of some claimants to decide what their needs were...Would you see a role for social workers in that? (Quotations are from the transcript of the SB Review Seventh Oral Hearing, 1 October 1984).

Superficially, it may seem that there would be certain advantages in such an arrangement. In certain limited circumstances, adjudication officers are already able to accept social workers' recommendations : this idea would considerably extend that principle. Surely it would help to secure DHSS cash and protect 'Section 1' and analogous budgets? In fact, even at the crude cash level, there would be considerable hazards: within the complex world of central government subsidies to LAs, spending penalties and the like, it is very probable that LAs would end up with an extra financial burden, through extra staffing, which would rebound on other budgets – including 'Section 1'. While at the level of principle, the dangers of social workers' administering locally assessed poor relief on a growing scale should be clear to anybody with any knowledge of the historical antecedents.

Thus, this hearing was seen by the AMA team as an opportunity to give an early 'thumbs down' to such lines of thinking. As Toby Harris put it:

> We feel very strongly that it would be wrong to shift the boundary further back into the direction of local authorities and say that they will have a greater role in providing cash...When we are talking about income maintenance, whether it be special needs or whatever, we are talking about...a basic citizenship right.

I argued that the proposal (however tentative) tended

> to imply that people who are having difficulties...have special needs. I doubt that that is the case. The problem is that people have not got enough money...To suggest that they should have assessments done by social workers would create a lot of problems. Many claimants do not have social workers and do not want them. The only problem is that they do not have enough money.

Mr Newton's worrying scenario has, of course, survived in the 'social fund' proposal: social workers will ignore the implications of this at their peril.

Thus, this 'frontiers' question plods on, causing headaches for all concerned, not least claimants. I trust that the above will have illustrated the wide range of levels and types of action which are appropriate to attempts to tackle it.

I would like now to adopt a rather different angle of view on the question of 'taking-up wider issues', and look at the scope for undertaking work jointly with claimants.

Joint action with claimants

I am aware that the question of working with consumers/claimants/clients takes us into a very wide area of debate going far beyond the scope of this book, whether we are considering particular 'categories' of claimant (say, hostel-dwellers) or claimants in particular geographical localities. I do not intend to attempt a potted history of community action: suffice it to say that welfare rights work has a close historical affinity with this area of activity. While we can ascribe the development of the modern advice centre to a great extent to the proliferation of citizens' advice bureaux during the Second World War, the more combative, partisan, and avowedly pro-claimant approach to welfare rights, strongly influenced by developments in the United States, grew up in the 1960s and 1970s, linked to the Community Development Projects and the activities of claimants' unions and other types of self-help group. (For more remote historical antecedents, see for example the account given by the Supplementary Benefits Commission – 1977, appendix C, pp.240—1 – of 'organised demands' on the offices of the Unemployment Assistance Board in the 1930s.)

Local authority welfare rights workers tend to support the idea of joint action with claimants' groups as one means of avoiding the development of paternalistic relationships as a result of the mystique of expertise in a complex area. Community workers of course have a continuing close contact with this range of issues. Social workers on the other hand may need to overcome traditional notions of individual casework in order to make progress: but there is no reason why any of the initiatives described below should not be mounted by a social work team.

Strathclyde Welfare Rights Service has laid a good deal of emphasis on this approach to welfare rights work. For example, the following description (by Quintin Oliver, the then divisional welfare rights adviser for Glasgow) of work with chronically sick and disabled claimants and their families, focused on day centres and adult training centres, strikes the right balance of active intervention without notions of superiority or condescension:

> It had...some interesting political repercussions. We met the parents of mentally and physically handicapped clients in the centres themselves. Most of the relatives had never been to the centres before and there was a transformation in them after we had sorted out their benefits. They became much more bolshy about their general rights to be involved in the care of their children and the centre's management. We would not boast about organising the parents' group – we just assisted in an eye-opening exercise and a confidence-booster. (Quoted in Sharron, 1982, pp.8—9)

Another example of welfare rights work where claimants

acted as partners of advisers and not as passive recipients of help is provided by the Glasgow 'hostels campaign', details of which have been published by the Campaign for Single Homeless People, CHAR (Oliver, 1983). Again, the advisers in question were WROs employed by Strathclyde Regional Council's Social Work Department, but there would be nothing to prevent other relevant social services staff pursuing similar lines of action. To summarise a long and complex tale, hostel dwellers were found to be suffering underpayments on a considerable scale, in respect of basic supplementary benefit entitlement, additional requirements, single payments and inadequately formulated meals allowances. A large-scale claiming exercise was mounted which led to negotiations between the DHSS and Strathclyde Regional Council and the securing of increased benefits and arrears payments running into very large figures (Oliver provisionally estimates '£1 million back-money and £1 millon per year extra payments').

Oliver further notes that:

It was especially encouraging among this traditionally alienated and deprived group that the residents seized upon the chance of campaigning around their individual and collective interests. A Welfare Rights Committee sprang up drawing elected representatives from each hostel, reporting back and spreading information on progress and developments. Concerned that the DHSS might be stalling, a picket was mounted...a deputation marched to see the local manager who promised there would be no further prevarication.

Once DHSS had conceded the benefits, the hostels committee moved on to 'support and advice on banking and spending the large arrears payments...Now they are moving on again to the remaining outstanding issues of rehousing and health'. The self-generation of self-respect and enthusiasm is clear:

Organising for the pickets and deputations was a novel undertaking for most of those involved and was pursued eagerly; especially when the media at first responded so well, characterising their struggle as the dispossessed against the state. When the final success came they delegated their chosen representatives to speak but were bitterly disappointed at the headlines of the press, reacting strongly against the images of dosser and tramp. In fact the arrears payments have represented a boon to many, providing the means to escape from hostel life.

The nadir of the more negative press coverage was perhaps represented by the *News of the World's* 'Tramps Hit the Jackpot'. While this represents a relatively thoughtful headline for this section of Fleet Street ('jackpot', for example, has two syllables) nevertheless it illustrates the hostile stereotypes too often peddled by the mass media. The problems presented by anti-welfare ideology are discussed further below.

This considerable local success was not seen by the WROs concerned as the end of the story:

> local issues and individual anomalies can be elevated to national questions with national answers. Already the results of this exercise have been reported to the national Welfare Rights Officers' Group and, by this briefing, to CHAR members. The DHSS in Edinburgh is known to have agreed to a similar reassessment of all its hostellers on the same basis and others are pressing claims as part of a national campaign. (All quotations from Oliver, 1983, pp.4—6)

For a further example, I shall return to Newcastle upon Tyne, where the 'McCutcheons Court' project secured considerable gains for claimants, acting in collaboration with WROs and with help from social workers.

McCutcheons Court consists of ten, five-storey blocks in the East End of Newcastle, an area of high and rising unemployment on the Tyne's declining shipyard belt. The Court suffers from problems of cheap construction, damp, old and expensive electric heating, lack of insulation and an exposed situation on the edge of the river : heating problems are thus guaranteed. The Tenants' Action Group was formed in May 1983. It has pursued questions of heating equipment, insulation and other problems, but high fuel bills have emerged as the most important issue. There is high unemployment in the blocks and many tenants are on supplementary benefit, but the DHSS took the line that additional requirements for heating did not exist.

In the summer of 1983, a tenant approached the Welfare

Rights Service, having had a claim for an additional requirement rejected. It seemed to the WROs in the area that a concerted effort on behalf of all tenants potentially entitled would be more appropriate than the pursuit of isolated cases. Discussions were entered into with the Tenants' Action Group and a joint take-up campaign was mounted, focusing on additional requirements for heating, but seeking out other entitlements also.

A sympathetic solicitor endeavoured unsuccessfully to obtain funding under the legal advice and assistance scheme for a technical survey of the flat involved in the initial appeal. The Area Housing Management Group was then approached and agreed to fund a survey by the City Architect's Department. The report of this survey confirmed that the heating system was inadequate and that the flats were 'exceptionally difficult to heat as presently constructed'. Armed with this evidence, the campaign went on to pursue claims for the higher rate of heating addition (then £ 5.05 per week) on the grounds that the flats were exceptionally difficult to heat adequately. Additional requirements awards for extra laundry costs were also pursued, on the grounds that the flats had no suitable washing or drying facilities. A standard claim form was designed and training sessions for the Tenants' Action Group were provided by the WROs. The tenants and WROs, with the help of social workers from the local SSD area office, then went 'door-knocking' and duly generated over 80 claims.

The initial DHSS response was to turn down claims, but upon being presented with the report of the technical survey, the local office decided to pay the lower rate of heating addition (then £2.05 per week) to all claimants in the blocks. This was not acceptable to the tenants, and appeals were launched, WROs representing at hearings. Ten appeal hearings later, the DHSS's confidence in its stance was wilting – all ten had been won by the tenants. The higher rate addition for all relevant tenants was conceded.

The gains were substantial: an estimated approximate gain (at 1983/4 benefit rates) of £35 000 in heating additions, with £26 000 arrears; £3250 in other additions, with £2500 arrears; and £3000 in single payments. In the words of the project report, this exercise 'shows that it is possible for tenants to organise together with professional workers and campaign for their rights' (McCutcheons Court Tenants' Action Group, Newcastle Tenants' Federation and Newcastle Welfare Rights Service, 1984, p.1).

I would like to conclude this part of this chapter with a good example of how *not* to work with claimants' groups. In order not to reactivate friction and embarrassment, I shall keep anonymous the LA area in question; although it is interesting to note that the area social services team concerned had a previous record of some quite imaginative community-orientated work, and seems here to have suffered an unexpected lapse. The case again concerns a dilapidated housing development, which we shall call 'Dampfields'. This estate was so eminently in need of a tenants' association that the absence of one became a significant cause for concern amongst a wide range of agencies, not only in the immediate locality, but amongst housing interests in general in the town in question. In due course, interested individual tenants linked up with several concerned agencies – a local community work project; the local advice centre; two housing rights groups (one of them itself a tenants' group); and the local social services area team – to launch a tenants' association. This body soon gathered strength and the involvement of the tenants themselves reached the point where a highly successful benefit take-up campaign was run by them in partnership with the local advice centre and with some helpful but modest involvement by the local social services area team.

So far, so good : but unfortunately, at this point, the social services team, or a member or members thereof, seems to have been overcome by a desire to celebrate its community involvement to the extent of promoting its own role and playing down that of others, including the community itself. A report was presented to the Social Services Committee which, to those not involved, sounded impressive:

> social work staff took the initiative...a project which is now run by and for the tenants...social work staff playing the role of enablers...objectives...to share the work of the tenants' association as colleagues rather than social workers and

clients...we have utilised groupwork skills and generally acted as enablers.

The other agencies involved in the various initiatives in the area were indignant. But the interesting point, or the essence of the cautionary tale, for our present purposes, is the reaction of the tenants. They felt patronised and angry. They approached the tenants' campaign group which had been one of those bodies involved in the association's foundation, and the local advice centre. A joint letter, of which I have acquired a copy, was duly sent to the social services area team leader, with copies to the Chairman and Director of Social Services:

> We are concerned that your report does not pay due justice to the work of other organisations in the initiatives in Dampfields and in particular, seriously underplays the role played by the tenants themselves in the setting up and work of the tenants' association...It is certainly correct to say that social work staff were involved in the early stages of the group but the initiative to start a group came not from them but from the tenants themselves. Many organisations were involved...There is, unfortunately, no mention of the role of these agencies in your report. Similarly with the take-up campaign...anyone reading your report could be forgiven for forming the impression that this campaign was mounted by yourselves and the DHSS. In fact it was initiated, planned and conducted jointly by the tenants' association and the advice centre...we are...annoyed that your report seeks to present the picture that your staff played the leading role in the work that has been done in Dampfields...This is not the case. The social work team has been one of many organisations involved in supporting the tenants' association. But the primary factor in the initiatives made in Dampfields has been the tenants themselves – without their involvement and enthusiasm none of the work done by yourselves or any of the other services would have come to anything. (These extracts are quoted unaltered except for the removal of names of agencies and of the locality.)

The implications of this for the practice of community-orientated social work are profound. If claimants/clients/tenants/consumers are really to be partners, then the mutual respect must be genuine. It is no use transposing into a 'community' guise the paternalistic and patronising relationships which characterise the worst aspects of traditional casework.

I would like to turn now to the final aspect of this discussion of 'wider issues' in welfare rights as practised within the social services : that of anti-welfare ideology and the importance of social services professionals putting their weight behind efforts to combat it.

Combating anti-welfare ideology

The British social security system did not appear from nowhere : it has its roots in the Poor Law. Nor do the attacks upon it, or the continuing legitimation of its deficiencies, spring out of thin air : the sturdy beggar, the spiv, the sponger, the scrounger, all have a long political history and – like anything which lasts – have a real practical role to play (see Golding and Middleton, 1982). If we are serious about making progress, we must confront the ideological trappings of anti-welfare interests. Nor are the systems of ideas which protect the status quo confined to crude and negative sterotyping of claimants : there are other, powerful notions, such as 'the nation can't afford it' which come dressed as economic theories and which have a mesmerising effect on many who would otherwise support an attack on poverty and the reform of social security.

I do not intend to relate here any particular success or substantial piece of work, but rather, given that this book is directed largely at a social services readership, would like to float some ideas concerning the role which social services professionals might play.

In November 1983, I attended a conference in Dundee entitled, 'Towards a Coherent Policy for Disadvantaged Children', organised by the Association for Family Therapy, the National Children's Bureau, and Dundee University's Department of Extra-Mural Education. The conference brought together a wide range of professionals from the health, education, housing and personal social services. It focused on themes arising from the findings of the National Child Development Study (Prosser and Wedge, 1973; Essen and Wedge, 1982a, 1982b) and on the various dimensions of poverty as it afflicts children. I had been invited to speak on income maintenance, and for two reasons I decided to make the combating of anti-welfare ideology one of my main themes. The first reason was premeditated : it seemed to me that here was gathered a very considerable body of collective experience of the different manifestations of poverty – all people who were in a position to make a weighty contribution to the public debate. The second reason emerged on the day : although *income* and *housing* had been clearly identified, not least by the main speaker, Peter Wedge, as central elements in disadvantage amongst children, I had the impression that conference members tended to feel that these problems were too enormous for them, personally, to be able to do much about them. Thus, while the main problems were clearly identified, the detailed discussions – which, I should stress, were informed and constructive – tended nevertheless to skirt round the ankles of these two social policy giants.

Part of my task was to set out in outline the sort of programme in the income maintenance field which will be required if poverty is seriously to be tackled : benefits to be paid at an adequate level; to be non-means-tested and non-contribution-tested; child benefit to be improved, to overtake and replace other children's benefits; a statutory minimum wage to be introduced; benefits to be paid on the basis of individual assessment, to free women from financial dependence on men; carers to be brought adequately into the benefit system, linked to a policy on adequate care services; the tax system to be correspondingly reformed, both to link with and to finance the benefit system. Such a programme is expensive and might well be written off as desirable but unattainable unless prevailing notions as to what the nation can afford can be dispersed. A second part of my task, then, was to try to offer some suggestions on this question of generating the public support and political will to alter the distribution of resources. The arguments I employed at the conference are summarised below : they are intended to persuade the social services professional not to be too pessimistic concerning the possibilities for change. The conventionally encouraged view is at a crude level that claimants do not deserve a better benefits system; and at a more sophisticated level, that society cannot afford it anyway. I do not have space here for an extensive discussion of 'scroungerism' but I suspect, and certainly hope, that its grip on the public imagination is weakening as more and more members of that public, and their families and friends, themselves join the 'scrounging' throng. Let us hope that such memories prove lasting if and when employment revives.

As regards what can and cannot be afforded : this debate tends to confuse two different questions – the size of the cake; and the way that we cut it. Economic policy is undoubtedly important, but we must not allow it to distract us from the question of the distribution and redistribution of incomes. We need to restructure the tax system and also establish minimum and maximum incomes. Essen and Wedge (1982a, p.94), call for 'a clear commitment by politicians and all concerned about disadvantage to the improvement of children's and families' circumstances'. How can we achieve such a 'clear commitment' and how do we persuade people to be 'concerned about disadvantage'?

Attitudes to these questions will vary between different societies (Rabier and Riffault, 1977) but certainly in Britain, there is a profound ambivalence. This is a result of the different ideological streams which feed into British public attitudes. On the one hand, there is the capacity for social solidarity in the face of adversity, such as prevailed in the wartime and immediate post-war period in the 1940s. On the other, there is the spirit of individual selfishness and personal gain in the context of the consumer society. The latter element will of course link easily with the legacy of the Poor Law in influencing the attitudes of the 'haves' towards the 'have nots'. The British public is capable of espousing any of these different ideological elements at different times and to different degrees. In such a position of ambivalence, it is essential for anti-poverty interests to use all available channels to tip the balance in the direction of social responsibility. Otherwise, there will be *no suitable political context* for change, and all our research and analysis of the problems will achieve little.

There are, it seems, some grounds for hope. The London Weekend TV/MORI 'Breadline Britain' survey found in 1983 that: 76 per cent agreed that differences in pay between the highly and lowly paid are too great; 63 per cent are in favour of higher taxes on the rich; 74 per cent thought the gap between rich and poor is too wide; 66 per cent supported the introduction of a minimum wage; 74 per cent would be prepared to pay more tax to enable everyone to afford necessities (Lansley and Mack, 1983, pp.12—13). Public opinion is perhaps not so hostile as we are often led to believe, or as the Rabier and Riffault study (1977) suggested it was in the mid-1970s. Thus, I argued at the Dundee conference that social services professionals, in all the varied fields represented there, 'could and should use all appropriate platforms, whether they be professional; trade union; political party; voluntary organisation; the media; or a conversation in the bus queue about "scroungers" ' (Fimister, 1984a, p.29).

With growing unemployment and the sort of public concern reflected in the 'Breadline Britain' findings, is it too much to hope that now might well prove to be a good time to achieve decisive changes in public and political attitudes? As one celebrated social commentator put it, a long time ago: 'There is a tide in the affairs of men which, taken at the flood, leads on to fortune' (Shakespeare, 1623, *Julius Caesar*, Act4, Scene 3). Claimants do not need a fortune: a decent income would suffice.

8

Conclusions

I have argued in this book that welfare rights work is of growing relevance to a wide range of social services staff, given the income problems faced by large and growing numbers of social services clients. I have considered at some length, in Chapter 2, the arguments concerning the place of welfare rights within social work and have attempted to trace the main elements in a detailed debate concerning how prescriptive one can be in urging welfare rights methods upon social workers. I have concluded that, wherever one stands on this question, there must be minimum standards of welfare rights knowledge, and that the complex nature of social security means that these minimum levels are in fact higher than many perhaps realise. I have summarised a substantial body of action research which demonstrates the gains to be made for clients when welfare rights methods are deployed.

If social services agencies are to take this question seriously, then it must be added that adequate resources must be made available to staff. This includes well-run information systems; and training programmes designed to tackle the subject effectively. The issues surrounding these have been set out in Chapters 5 and 6. A welfare rights resource of some kind is needed in each area if the necessary back-up facilities are to be provided: Chapters 3 and 4 consider in some detail the options and the political context of efforts to secure such resources.

I have used Bull's concept of an 'advocacy continuum' to help us consider not only the role of welfare rights within social work, but also the questions surrounding 'cause advocacy' − the taking-up of wider issues arising from work on individual cases. I have considered cause advocacy, in Chapter 7, in terms of lobbying activities; of work with claimants' groups; and of the wider question of tackling anti-welfare ideology.

A recurring theme has of course been the low levels of social security and welfare benefits and the poverty so frequently associated with them. A closely related theme is the exacerbation of this situation by the manifestly large-scale failure of the system to ensure that claimants receive their entitlements. Moreover, both those who do receive their full, if meagre, ration, and those who do not, are likely to face the complexities of elaborate, cumbersome and confusing legal provisions and bureaucratic rules and structures. This last problem area (that of complexity) has perhaps not so far received quite as much emphasis here as it should, so I would like to devote a little space in these closing pages to this particular aspect of the multi-faceted problems which welfare rights work is designed to confront.

Complexity, in its various forms, in fact does not derive at root from a lack of official imagination : often, it stems from the fundamental nature of social security provision as we have it at present. For example, the cohabitation rule, which operates in several areas of the benefit system, owes its existence to assumptions about women's dependence on men. The tangle of disablement benefits derives from the failure of society to put up the money for a unified system. The most notable case of all is the supplementary benefit system itself. Not only does mass dependence on supplementary benefit derive substantially from under-investment in non-means-tested benefits; but even within the SB system, many complexities – including aspects of the additional requirements and single payments rules; and complex 'direct payment' and debt-collecting provisions – can be seen to derive from the low level of the basic benefit rates.

In Chapter 7, I presumed to invoke Shakespeare in support of my argument. But a name more usually associated with the world of social security is that of the twentieth-century writer, Franz Kafka. Earlier in Chapter 7, I quoted a *Social Work Today* reader from Hackney as describing the social security system as 'Kafkaesque'. Some would say that this is no exaggeration, so I once put the matter to the test, in CPAG's *Welfare Rights Bulletin* (Fimister, 1984b, pp.6—7), by means of a couple of case studies. For those readers who do not regularly read the specialist welfare rights press, I shall repeat the exercise here:

Case 1 Ms B, a single parent, has been notified that she has rent arrears of £497 for a previous council tenancy (she is now a housing association tenant). During the previous tenancy she was on supplementary benefit, and should have had 100 per cent housing benefit. A phone call to the Housing Department reveals that the housing benefit certificate was retrospectively cancelled – reason not known. Phone call to the DHSS explaining this. They confirm that the certificate was cancelled apparently in error, and they will issue a further certificate. Phone call to Housing Department to tell them this. Memo sent to City Treasurer's Department (who are pursuing the arrears) explaining the position, and asking them to take no action pending receipt of the duplicate certificate. Two weeks later phone call to Housing Department – duplicate certificate not received. Phone call to the DHSS. Duplicate was issued, but they will now issue further duplicate. Three weeks later, the second duplicate has not been received. Letter to DHSS Assistant Manager asking for further certificate. Reply from DHSS – having issued two duplicate certificates, they are not prepared to issue another without written confirmation from the Housing Department that previous certificates have not been received. (They state that they have had confirmation from the Civic Centre of receipt of the batch of certificates). Memo sent to Housing Department with a copy of DHSS letter, asking for thorough check, and written confirmation of non-receipt, if this is in fact the case. Reply currently awaited.

Case 2 But this reply doesn't appear to have reached the original department... but by mistake went to another Department, B. So Department A remained without an answer, but unfortunately our full reply didn't reach B either; whether it was that the order itself was not enclosed by us, or whether it got lost on the way – it was certainly not lost in my department, that I can vouch for – in any case all that arrived at Department B was the covering letter... Meanwhile Department A was waiting for our answer: they had, of course, made a memorandum of the case, but as excusably enough often happens and is bound to happen even under the most efficient handling, our correspondent trusted to the fact that we would answer him... As a result he never thought of referring to his memorandum and the whole thing fell into oblivion.

Case 1 is from case notes provided by Diane Jones, a WRO in Newcastle. Case 2 is from Chapter 5 o f *The Castle,* by Kafka

(1926). There is a further twist: I discovered recently that Kafka was, in his youth, a clerk at the Workers' Insurance Office in Prague – so it may well be that the social security system of his day had some formative influence on his insights.

I trust that I have said enough to emphasise the point made at the beginning of Chapter 7 : that our income maintenance systems are as much part of the problem as of the solution, all of which adds further force to the argument that a comprehensive approach to welfare rights, tackling policy issues as well as individual cases, is to be preferred. In fact, the two approaches are interdependent : policy-orientated work amplifies the impact of welfare rights casework; while the gathering of evidence, understanding of the problems and achievement of credibility which are necessary for policy work are dependent on a real-life knowledge of what is actually going on 'out there'.

I would like to return finally to my argument that every social services agency should have, or have access to, a welfare rights unit of some sort. If I had to choose one main practical suggestion to direct towards policy-makers, that would be it. The conditions of the 1980s – poverty, unemployment, the growing problems of social security – present a tremendous challenge to the personal social services. Social services agencies must be both willing, and equipped, to meet it.

References

NB. items listed in Chapter 5 ('information systems') are not repeated here unless they also occur in other contexts.

Ballantyne, A. (1984) 'Benefit accruing from consulting a computer' (news item) *Guardian*, 13 August.

Barclay, P. (Chairman) (1982) *Social Workers: their Role and Tasks*, London, Bedford Square Press.

Barter, J. (1973a) 'Comment on welfare rights', *Social Work Today*, vol. 4, no. 13, 20 September.

Barter, J. (1973b) Letter in *Social Work Today*, vol.4, no.16, 15 November.

Becker, S. (1983) 'Social workers' involvement with welfare rights and advocacy', Nottingham, MA/CQSW thesis, Dept of Social Administration and Social Work, University of Nottingham.

Becker, S., MacPherson, S. and Silburn, R. (1983) *Saints, Ferrets and Philosophers: Social Workers and Supplementary Benefits*, Nottingham, Benefits Research Unit, Dept of Social Administration and Social Work, University of Nottingham.

Bennett, T. (Senior Welfare Rights Adviser, Harlow) (1984a) Letter to the author, 23 March.

Bennett, T. (1984b) 'Getting more money for your clients: a duty', 'Benefits', *Social Work Today*, vol.16, no.6, 8 October.

Bennett, T. (1985) Telephone conversation with the author, 27 February.

Bennett, T. and McGavin, P. (1980a) 'Benefiting from good advice', *Community Care*, 31 July.

Bennett, T. and McGavin, P. (1980b) Letters, *Community Care*, 2 October.

Birmingham Citizens' Advice Bureau (1981) *Local Advice Needs in the Birmingham Inner City Partnership Area*, Birmingham CAB.

Blunn, C. and Small, M. (1984) 'The anomalies of attendance allowance', *Community Care*, 16 February.

Bridge, B. and Campling, J. (1978) *Employment Problems: the Social Work Involvement*, Birmingham, British Association of Social Workers.

Brighton Welfare Rights Campaign (1982) *Brighton Welfare Rights Campaign Report*, Brighton, BWRC.

British Association of Social Workers (1975) *A Code of Ethics for Social Work*, Birmingham, BASW.

British Association of Social Workers (1984) Resolution adopted at Annual General Meeting.

Brooke, R. (1973) 'Which way for welfare rights teaching?', *Social Work Today*, vol.4, no.13, 20 September.

Bull, D. (1970) 'Action for welfare rights', in *The Fifth Social Service: a Critical Analysis of the Seebohm Proposals*, London, Fabian Society.

Bull, D. (1980) 'The anti-discretion movement in Britain: fact or phantom?', *Journal of Social Welfare Law*, March.

Bull, D. (1982a) *Welfare Advocacy: Whose Means to What Ends?*, text of Sheila Kay Memorial Lecture, Birmingham, British Association of Social Workers.

Bull, D. (1982b) 'Social worker as advocate?', *Social Work Today*, vol.14, no.14, 7 December.

Burgess, P. (1973) 'Rights man in welfare', *New Society*, 13 September.

Burgess, P. (1983) 'In benefit', *Community Care*, 10 February.

Cambridgeshire Information and Advice Services Working Party (1980) *A Review of Information and Advice Services in Cambridgeshire*, Cambridgeshire IASWP.

Campbell, A. (1977) 'The importance of a certain section', *Community Care*, 4 May.

Campling, J. (1980) 'Social work for the out of work', *Social Work Today*, vol.12, no.14, 2 December.

Casserly, J. and Clark, B. (1978) *A Welfare Rights Approach to the Chronically Sick and Disabled*, Strathclyde Regional Council.

Check! Rights Centre (1977) *Final Report 1977*, London, British Association of Settlements and Social Action Centres.

Child Poverty Action Group (1984) *Welfare Rights Training Courses: Let our Experience Work for You*, leaflet, London, CPAG.

City of Newcastle upon Tyne (1982) *High Unemployment in the Inner City: the Impact on Local Government and the Community*, Policy Services Dept, City of Newcastle upon Tyne.

Clark, B., Daly, J. and Douglas, J. (1984) *Nobody's Benefit: a Survey of the Housing Benefit Scheme*, London, Child Poverty Action Group.

Cohen, R. (1983) *Able to Claim?: a Report of Work with Occupational Therapists and Physiotherapists to Improve Take-up of Disability Benefits*, London, Islington People's Rights.

Cohen, R. and Rushton, A. (1982) *Welfare Rights*, London, Heinemann/ *Community Care*.

Cohen, R. and Tarpey, M. (1982) *The Trouble with Take-up: a Report of Work with Social Services to Increase Take-up of Social Security Benefits*, London, Islington People's Rights.

Cypher, J. and Walton, R. (1973) 'Welfare rights and social work education', *Social Work Today*, vol.4, no.13, 20 September.

Davies, M. (1984) 'Training: what we think of it now', *Social Work Today*, 24 January.

Davis, A. (1984) 'Help on the Hill', *Social Work Today*, vol.15, no.40, 18 June.

Department of Health and Social Security (1979) *Relations with Social Services: Report of a Joint Study by the Department's Regional Directorate and Social Work Service of the Relationships between the Supplementary Benefits Organisation and Social Services*, London, DHSS.

Emett, T. and Lister, R. (1976) *Under the Safety Net*, London, Child Poverty Action Group.

Equality for Children (1983) *Keeping Kids Out of Care: Crisis and Consensus in Childcare Policy*, London, Equality for Children.

Essen, J. and Wedge, P. (1982a) *Children in Adversity*, London, Pan.

Essen, J. and Wedge, P. (1982b) *Continuities in Childhood Disadvantage*, London, Heinemann.

Etherington, S. (1984) 'Handing out a crumb of comfort', *Social Work Today*, vol.16, no.7, 15 October.

Fimister, G. (1977) *Exceptional Needs Payment or 'Section One' Payment?: the Development of One City's Policy*, Newcastle Welfare Rights Service, City of Newcastle upon Tyne.

Fimister, G. (1979a) 'Constructing a local poverty lobby', *Social Work Today*, vol.11, no.5, 2 October.

Fimister, G. (1979b) 'Local authority welfare rights workers: pay survey 1979', unpublished survey findings, Newcastle Welfare Rights Service, City of Newcastle upon Tyne.

Fimister, G. (1979c) *Looking Over the Fence: a Response to the DHSS Document, 'Relations with Social Services'*, Newcastle Welfare Rights Service, City of Newcastle upon Tyne.

Fimister, G. (1980a) 'A working guide to the new SB scheme', 'For your client's benefit', *Social Work Today*, vol.12, no.13, 25 November.

Fimister, G. (1980b) 'Frontier problems', in Coussins, J. (ed.), *Dear SSAC: an Open Letter to the Social Security Advisory Committee*, London, Child Poverty Action Group.

Fimister, G. (1981a) *Income Rights: the Advice Network in Newcastle upon Tyne*, Newcastle Welfare Rights Service, City of

Newcastle upon Tyne.

Fimister, G. (1981b) 'A guided tour of the welfare rights maze', 'For your client's benefit', *Social Work Today*, vol.12,no.38, 9 June.

Fimister, G. (1984a) 'The importance of constructive reform versus anti-welfare ideology', in De'Ath, E. and Hill, M. (eds), *Towards a Coherent Policy for Disadvantaged Children*, Dundee, Association for Family Therapy/National Children's Bureau/Dept of Extra-Mural Education, University of Dundee.

Fimister, G. (1984b) 'Like Kafka', *Welfare Rights Bulletin*, no.59, Child Poverty Action Group.

Golding, P. and Middleton, S. (1982) *Images of Welfare: Press and Public Attitudes to Poverty*, London, Martin Robertson.

Hannah, A. (Regional Welfare Rights Officer, Lothian) (1985) Conversation with the author, 2 March.

Hayward, W., Julia, A. and Morgan, P. (1977) 'In practice', *Community Care*, 16 November.

Hill, M. and Laing, P. (1978) *Money Payments, Social Work and Supplementary Benefits: a Study of Section One of the 1963 Children and Young Persons Act*, Bristol, School for Advanced Urban Studies, University of Bristol.

Holman, R. (1973) 'Poverty, welfare rights and social work', *Social Work Today*, vol.4, no.12, 6 September.

Holman, R. (1980) *Inequality in Child Care*, 2nd edn, London, Child Poverty Action Group/Family Rights Group.

Howard, A. (1978) *Welfare Rights: the Local Authorities' Role*, London, Bedford Square Press.

Kafka, F. (1926) *The Castle*, various editions, first published Berlin.

Kemp, P. (1984) *The Cost of Chaos: a Survey of the Housing Benefit Scheme*, London, SHAC.

Lancaster, E. (1984) 'Someone to lean on', 'Benefits', *Social Work Today*, 3 January.

Lansley, S. and Mack, J. (1983) *Breadline Britain : the Findings of the Television Series*, London Weekend Television. (And, more recently, Lansley and Mack (1985) *Poor Britain*, London, Allen & Unwin).

Lister, R. (1977) 'Dear David Donnison: the frontier problem that won't go away', *Social Work Today*, vol.8, no.31, 10 May.

Liverpool Welfare Rights Resource Centre (1982) *Save Liverpool Welfare Rights*, leaflet, Liverpool, LWRRC.

Lynes, T. (1970) 'Welfare rights', in *The Fifth Social Service: a Critical Analysis of the Seebohm Proposals*, London, Fabian Society.

Lynes, T. (1981) *The Penguin Guide to Supplementary Benefits*, 4th edn. Harmondsworth, Penguin. (The ref. in the text is to the 1981 edn; a 1985 edn is also available).

Lynes, T. (1985) Telephone conversation with the author, 9 April.

McCutcheons Court Tenants' Action Group, Newcastle Tenants' Federation and Newcastle Welfare Rights Service (1984) *McCutcheons Court: a Campaign for Extra Money for Heating*, Newcastle upon Tyne, McCutcheons Court TAG/NTF/NWRS.

McGrail, S. (1983a) *Survey into the Teaching of Welfare Rights on Postgraduate CQSW Courses in the United Kingdom*, Stirling, Dept of Sociology, University of Stirling.

McGrail, S. (1983b) 'We shouldn't really be teaching this sort of thing', *Community Care*, 15 December.

McKnight, J. (1985) 'Pressure points: the crisis in management', in Ward, S. (ed.), *DHSS in Crisis: Social Security – Under Pressure and Under Review*, London, Child Poverty Action Group.

Melotte, C. (1977) 'Testing knowledge of welfare rights', *Social Work Today*, vol.8, no.35, 14 June.

Moore, P. (1980) 'Counter-culture in a social security office', *New Society*, 10 July.

National Association of Citizens' Advice Bureaux (1984) *Housing Benefit: the Cost to the Claimant*, London, NACAB.

National Consumer Council (1977) *The Fourth Right of Citizenship: a Review of Local Advice Services*, London, NCC.

National Consumer Council (1982) *Who Knows?: Guidelines for a Review of Local Advice and Information Services and How to Publicise Them*, London, NCC.

Oliver, Q. (1983) *Maladministration of Benefits: the Glasgow Hostels Campaign*, London, CHAR.

Oliver, Q. (former Divisional Welfare Rights Adviser for Glasgow, Strathclyde Regional Council) (1984) Various communications with the author.

Parsloe, P. and Stevenson, O. (1978) *Social Work Area Teams: the Practitioner's View*, London, HMSO.

Pinker, R. (1979) 'Slimline social work', *New Society*, 13 December.

Prosser, H. and Wedge, P. (1973) *Born to Fail?*, London, Arrow.

Rabier, J-R. and Riffault, H. (1977) *The Perception of Poverty in Europe*, Brussels, Commission of the European Communities.

Richards, M. (1984), 'Pulled in all directions', *Community Care*, 18 October.

Rose, H. (1973), 'Who can de-label the claimant?: welfare rights from the claimant's perspective', *Social Work Today*, vol.4, no.13,   20 September.

Rush, P. (1984) 'HBAS made permanent', *Housing Benefits Campaign Bulletin*, no.4, Manchester, July.

Shakespeare, W. (1623) *Julius Caesar*, various editions, first published London. (The speech cited in the text was made by Brutus shortly before his downfall, so I would not wish to push the parallel too far.)

Sharkey, P. (1973) 'Welfare rights and social service departments', *Social Work Today*, vol.4, no.13, 20 September.

Sharron, H. (1982) 'Post and deliver', *Social Work Today*, vol.14,   no.14, 7 December.

Sheffield Information and Advice Services Working Party (1980) *Report on Information and Advice Service Provision in Sheffield*, Sheffield IASWP.

Simpson, T. (1978) *Advocacy and Social Change: a Study of Welfare Rights Workers*, London, National Institute for Social Work.

Slater, P. (1984) Letters, *Social Work Today*, vol.16, no.9, 29 October.

Smith, P. (1980) Letters, *Community Care*, 4 September.

Smith, R. (1981) *Evidence to the Barclay Committee*, London, Child Poverty Action Group.

Smith, R. (1982) 'Living in the material world', *Social Work Today*, vol.14, no.14, 7 December.

Smith, R. (1985) 'Who's fiddling?: fraud and abuse', in Ward, S.   (ed.), *DHSS in Crisis: Social Security - Under Pressure and Under Review*, London, Child Poverty Action Group.

Stevenson, O. (1973) *Claimant or Client?: a Social Worker's View of the Supplementary Benefits Commission*, London, Allen & Unwin.

Streather, J. (1972) 'Welfare rights and the social worker', *Social Work Today*, vol.3, no.13, 5 October.

Supplementary Benefits Commission (1977) *Report of the Supplementary Benefits Commission for the Year Ended 31 December 1976*, Cmnd. 6910, London, HMSO.

Watts, C. (1981) 'Honest brokers or agents of change?', *Social Work Today*, vol.12, no.49, 25 August.

Weir, S. (1984) *Parental Contributions for Children in Care: Proposals for a Fair System*, London, Family Rights Group.

Wellburn, R. (1984) Memo to the author, 31 May.

Wootton, B. (1959) *Social Science and Social Pathology*, London, Allen & Unwin.

Index